Marlburro Country

FILTER CIGARETTES

Marlburro

20 CLASS A CIGARETTES

G000155874

THE SURGEON GENERAL'S LAME ASS WARNING:
The Surgeon General has determined that smoking these high-test cigarettes to excess will not only give you an excessive case of burro breath, but: also turn your hooves excessively brown, your teeth excessively yellow, your lungs excessively black and make your nostril hairs smell like a campfire. - (Campfires don't have a very keen sense of smell, so be careful!)

Created, Written and Produced
by
THOMAS HAGEY

ART DIRECTION AND PRODUCTION
Kelvin Case

Text edited by Elizabeth Falkner

ANIMAL AND STUDIO PHOTOGRAPHY
Stan Switalski

STUDIO PHOTOGRAPHY
Steve Lawrence

ADDITIONAL PHOTOGRAPHY
Thomas Hagey

ASSEMBLY
Ken Hartley

ILLUSTRATION
Movies – David Prothero; Horse Tales – Anthony Jenkins;
TitHead – Michael Caunter; Hoofmekkler's People – David Loblaw;
Horse D'ouvres – Gail Walker; Hunt for Elvis – John Etheridge;
Prince Charles/Parting Shot/Air Heads/Aussie Rules – Kelvin Case;

Paper Sculpture – Ron Broda
Leather Sculpture – Brad Balch
Sculpture – Gary Walker
Cover and Spike Spurr Airbrushing: Bob Suzuki

TYPESETTING, SEPARATIONS AND FILM
Aurora Colour Imaging – Mississauga, Canada

Thanks to Minolta Canada – Ken Tatimichi

PROPS
Stanley Peter Owens, Heidi Brannan, Patrick Brannan, Shelley
MacFarlane, Don MacFarlane, Mike Melnychuk and Marilyn, Ken
Hartley, Kelvin Case.

CREATIVE SUGGESTIONS AND CREDITS
Helen Bridle, Lori Roy, Stan Switalski, Kent Heiden, John Stollery,
Allen Thomson, Kelvin Case.

**THANKS TO THE FOLLOWING HORSE PEOPLE, STABLES
AND RANCHES:**

Keith, Chris, Lee and Erin Murray, Ken and Joy Houston, Goleta
Valley Community Stables, Helsha Acuna, Checole Acuna, Yves
Garcia, Gerald, Jerry and Nancy Williams, Jack Miller, Colleen
McKenzie, C.S. Adams Stables, Suzy and Chamberlain Gentle
Mules, Cheryl Gibson, Flag Is Up Farms – Pat and Monty Roberts,
Karen Baucus, Prospect Farms and the Weldon Family, Jane Walker.

THANKS TO THE FOLLOWING HORSES:
Tic Tag Toe, Shady, Solay, Grasshopper (Pig)

THANKS TO THE FOLLOWING ASSES:
Poncho The Wonder Ass, The William's Sicilian Donkeys.

THANKS:
Heather Cameron, Eddy Pike, Kenny Young, The Duster, Drew Miller,
Freddy, Joanne Horsnell, Peter and Beth Becker, Blair and Audrey
Bender, Compact Sod Farms.

SPECIAL THANKS

William Wayne, Kent Heiden, Marsha Boulton, Wendy Davis, Sally,
Alex, Mary Jo, Shane, Laura, Frank, Helen Marie, Ron, Rob, Angie,
Andrea, Charlie, Lilly and Tim, Beirnes, Kim and Paul McAuley, Karen
Baucus, Jane Leis, Teresa McWilliams, Steve Melnychuk, Jim King,
Lynda Sowerby, Sandy Switalski, Glen Stemmler, Mary E. Lea, Reid
Bannister, The Lucinda Vardey Agency, Linda Turchin, Harry
Mathews, Peter Owens and Fanger, Keith Falkner, Shelly Lou
MacFarlane, Sherry MacFarlane, Betty Gallander, Eric and Banana
Hammock Marable – Hollywood Office, Cha Heiden, Sheelagh, My
family, Sandy Atkinson, My parents: Lloyd and the very lovely Bertha
May Hagey for their continuing love and support. Peter Butler,
everyone at Aurora, Kelvin Case, Ken Hartley and Hal.

TO THE FOLLOWING ESTABLISHMENTS:
Cafe 13 – Cambridge, Centro Grill and Wine Bar – The best
restaurant in the City of Toronto, Langdon Hall, Little River Inn,
Donut Gallery, Willy's Golden Bottle, Graystones, Hotel Holland
Centre – under the attentive care of Sally and Alex Beirnes.

Printed in the United States of America

First printing May, 1991

Bulk rates are available.

Published by: William Kent Inc. 201 N. Salsipuedes St., Suite 203,
Santa Barbara, California, USA 93103 Office: (805) 965-2408
Fax: (805) 962-4004

WK
WILLIAM
KENT
INCORPORATED
*The Humor
Publishers*

**The Best Of Penthorse is dedicated to the life, love, wisdom,
art and living spirit of, Robert Markle 1936-1990.**

THE BEST OF
PENTHORSE
BY THOMAS HAGEY

STABLE OF CONTENTS

Our Cover Mare – Wendy Houlihan.

EDITORIAL

By Bob Getchyerponi

(Founder of Penthorse Magazine, Worldwide Editor-in-chief)

These days, publications are judged by their content. Little is said about what they **don't** contain. I have yet to see a magazine yanked off the shelf for **not** having unsuitable, explicit subject matter. Yet **my** publication seems to be continuously under fire for exposing the truth . . . and a few bods and ends from the private sector. This annoys me to no end. Censorship. It's the worst kind of discrimination. Censorship is just one more way that the moral minority sinks its fangs into the necks of liberal-minded horses.

It is the duty of all Americans and really, all horses everywhere, to fight censorship. It is our constitutional right to read what we want, to view what we please. We cannot allow ourselves to be pushed around by a growing number of horses asses. The world is comprised of good and evil. Eliminate evil and good could get way out of control. Next thing you know everyone's saying, "Good morning", and actually meaning it and the result is: You end up with more horses asses than horses.

I write this editorial on the eve of our 25th anniversary – the night before the release of the Best Of Penthorse. And the *Best* of Penthorse it surely is. Best foot forward; always, that's Penthorse! We pride ourselves in knowing which foot comes first and which one comes next and who comes next after that and . . . Whew!! . . . God I like publishing skin books!

The truth is, if you keep reading Penthorse you'll end up knowing more than the moral minority. You *will* be able to tell the difference between your posterior and a hole in the ground.

I must confess, as founder, publisher and worldwide editor-in-chief, doing things my way has not been easy. It has indeed been a long haul but I've been fortunate enough to have accumulated a great deal of wisdom along the way. Wisdom which I want to share with my faithful readers right now in the form of a few helpful tips.

No, I said tips. (Tips does not have two "T"s in it!).

Bob's Helpful Tips (with a "P"!)

#1 Never pet a barking dog – even if he **is** wagging his tail.

#2 Never walk into an alleyway at night by yourself; especially not with a veterinarian or even a vegetarian!

#3 If you ever stop thinking that the only good politician is a dead politician, seek professional help.

#4 If you cater to the classes you'll eat with the masses. If you cater to the masses you'll eat with the classes. Don't forget it. It's how I became sexcessful.

#5 And last but by no means least: Never patronize a censor . . . unless she has nice breasts.

Hitler, Stalin and Castro would agree that censorship works. But at what cost? Freedom, of course.

This philosophy sounds sound. I mean I really sound sincere. I don't come off as though I'm merely playing up the freedoms issue to line my own tack box.

So what does this constant displaying of the south end of a filly walking north – for landslide profits – have to do with your individual stand on censorship? I'm not quite sure either. But I will promise you this: I'll get somebody on it right away and as soon as I find out the answer, you'll be the second to know.

Where Are All The Macho Studs?

Using advanced home renovation technology, Japanese know-how, and good old American ingenuity, STUDFINDER® takes the risk out of being close. Eliminating up to 99% of the bimbos with the push of a button.

I know it sounds like a breath mint or deodorant pitch, but it's not. Indeed, where are all the macho studs? Well, now with STUDFINDER®, they're never more than a stone's throw away. Read on!

If you're a concerned or lonely mare; a stallion who has a flair for both sides of the fence - or just tired of meeting Mr. Wrong -you need STUDFINDER®.

Simply aim it in any direction and hit the button. If you don't like what pops up on the screen, hit the button again. It's that simple!

STUDFINDER®...Bringing lovers together for over fifteen years and for under $49.00.

STUDFINDER®

From Simple Minds Come Simple Solutions!™

CALL ME MARE-DAM®

WITH
XAVIERA HOLLENTURF
THE DAFFY HOOKER

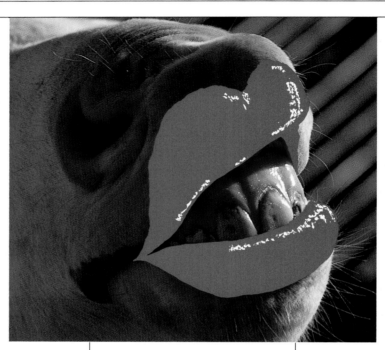

"You can lead a horse to water but you can't lead a horticulture"

Columnist's note:
Whoever dropped that quote off at the front door of this article obviously doesn't know much about prostitutes. I've been cultured most of my life! And you'll be as pleased as I was to know that often the tests came back negative.

Dear Xaviera Hollenturf: I've been reading your column since I was two years old. I was forever getting hoof prints all over the pages. Father would always know when I'd been snooping. I find it difficult to lick and turn pages at the same time. But I'll deal with that when the time comes.

Your career as a whore intrigues me. I must admit that I've enjoyed reading about your uninhibited escapades. But I do have several major questions.

If you've had sex with that many partners over the years:

1) Why aren't you dead by now from the sheer exhaustion? Not to mention all that sheer pantyhose; I swear it could eventually kill a horse. 2) Why haven't Sexually Transmitted Diseases killed you by now? 3) Isn't your vagina getting a little sore these days? If questions one and two don't *do* you in first, your vagina probably will, just for something *else* to do.

How does a prostitute keep *it* clean in the Age of Aids. Surely you don't take the time to hand wash, hang and drip dry "it" after every client. It would become rather tedious rather quickly. Have

you ever really thought about packing it in? (I'm sure you have but that's *not* what I was referring to.)

Ever considered retirement? Every athlete has his or her day and I dare say this has been at least the big marathon without the finish. But now that it's down to the wire do you honestly think you could stop doing the Old Baboomba for money long enough to take a holiday without doing the Old Baboomba to pay for your plane ticket, accommodation, etc. etc. You *will* need a real job sometime soon.

Perhaps legitimate of social work. I mean it's not like you can get endorsements from your style of vocation. I doubt that the Cozy Sleep® Mattress folks will come banging on your door at six o'clock in the morning (the police maybe) to get an on-camera testimonial – emphasis on the moan. They would, in turn, broadcast it live to their millions of shocked but attentive viewers:

"Over 700 hours without a squeak – from the mattress that is! Yes folks, it's truly a mattress that

can take a licking and a kicking (And several other things which I'd prefer not saying on public television). The Cozy Sleep® mattress; clearly a mattress you can trust. Cozy Sleep® . . . The mattress that more hookers prefer to use and use and use and use . . ."

Catch my drift? Why don't you quit while you're ahead. Hockey players hang up their skates. Baseball players hang up their gloves and spikes. Basketball players hang up their . . . their . . . balls? . . . Naaa! . . . That can't be right. They'd probably hang up their sneakers, too. Yes, that's it – sneakers. Maybe you should consider hanging up your vagina, so to speak. I mean, hell! You don't have to wash and fold it and put it in the cedar chest; just be good to it for a change.

I realize that this *is* your column and I'm eating up good paper right now and it isn't exactly: "Good morning! Talk to a hooker – you're on the air – Go ahead, caller!"

But if Roy Rogers can stuff Trigger, you can stuff your thingy once and for all – and nobody would be the wiser – at least not in *your* circle of friends. And given the numbers of replacement parts walking the streets these days, I don't think anyone will miss one hooker.

P.S. If half of what you write in your columns is true, and you've actually lived to tell, you've got major horseshoes up the ying yang! Consider your survival a small miracle and "get into" something else for a change.

NOT EVERYONE
UNDER THE SHEETS IN PENTHORSE
WANTS TO KISS YOU.

They say that love makes the world go 'round - but it's not all smootchie-wootchie out there. There are hate groups everywhere. Take the Klip Klop Klan (KKK) for instance. Spooky aren't they?

Each month, Penthorse magazine uncovers a lot more than pretty bodies. Our hard-hitting investigative reporting keeps you up to date on every aspect of the world of love and helps keep hate in its place: on the back roads, the bayous, and the secret meeting places of this great country of ours. You see, each issue of Penthorse also uncovers the TRUTH.

Every year our 16.5 million readers purchase 50 billion dollars worth of consumer goods. That's a lot of bits, bridles and saddles. (Yeah! But what *other* kind of consumer goods? Hmmm? No doubt the kind that take batteries ...) Okay! Okay! ... Bits, bridles, saddles AND vibrators ... and ah ... Yes, I suppose love gels. And I guess now that we're uncovering the TRUTH, there's probably another 6 billion in whips and chains that the government doesn't know about ... and ah ... okay French Ticklers ... and max, maybe another billion and a half in Whoopie Belts and Member Extenders.Well, now that the TRUTH is flowing, I may as well empty my other pocket! ...

Yes, ladies and gentlemen, aside from all the provocative talk, the revealing journalism, the titillating possibilities and the investigative lookin' each month - without fail - Penthorse is read by Horses who crave knowledge.

The knowledge that if they open up this magazine they can expect to see something shocking and, with any kind of luck at all, it won't be their wife, girlfriend or - heaven forbid - their little sister!

PENTHORSE
JUST SLIGHTLY MORE NAKED THAN THE TRUTH.

HE FLOOR!

Reebuck®

PENTHORSE FORUM

A Rendezvous Without Gratification
Letters?!? You want letters? . . . I'll give you a letter. You want to print something thought-provoking? How would you like to have a profession like mine?

I'm not asking for the world . . . All I want is a little bit . . . a little bit more of the time . . . or even just once!!!

This column is usually reserved for horny types of stories. I should know! I've read them a thousand times. My story is about arousal too, but the problem is: nothing ever gets done about it.

The letters which appear here describe firmness the way the word was meant to be described. They give the words . . . "throbbing and glistening in the noon-day sun" special significance. At least, special to *this* lonely horse.

It really takes it out of me even to read them, if you're a have not/get not like myself. They really take me

away from reality. Average horses never see life this way. You can escape from field and forest and pillars and posts and exercise rings. And *there* – free from ownership, but facing a slave's task – in a Best Western Hotel room or the romantic equivalent, on fresh, clovery, bleached sheets . . . the fantasy unfolds and comes alive before your very eyes. This fiction delivers the blow-by-blows – the exploits and escapades of some lucky horse with a name like Neville J. Steed. His love-acrobatics are performed flawlessly, roughly and rudely with perfect-bodied-Bridgettes-and-Tanya's (pronounced Tawn-ya!) who will do everything but dial the vet when they're through with you.

By through with you I mean you're spent! They've finished collapsing your lungs, jumping your bones, breaking your nose, yanking your mane *and* while they're there, you somehow succeed in permitting them to tear out your heart. They do it with unparalleled relish and professionalism.

Yet, to you they're not whores . . . or even bad. But they *are* – for sure – horses of a different color. If you were to broadloom the barn, they would be the color you'd choose from the PMS chart. Shags but not nags! The kind you sink into.

They leave you bruised, grateful and grinning. If you're conscious enough to realize you need medical attention and there's a phone in the barn (and you care enough at the time), you phone the vet. If you get the answering machine you happily but painfully chance another roll of the dice (pronounced Die!).

Sex does not happen the way it is portrayed in your magazine. At least, life is not this way for me. It is very fertile editorial and you have my full attention. However I find it difficult to relate. This is not *my* reality. I'm involved with what is commonly called as "The Big Tease". The farm where the have-nots, get not and therefore you expect not, that is all there is to that!

I'm the Bozo they bring in to see, IF SHE'S IN HEAT. It would be swell if I could quietly say, "Hi, are you getting close yet? They were just wondering and I know you're not going to let *me* anyway so why don't you just write your answer on a little piece of paper and I'll give it to them and then the stud will *give* it to you – instead of me – and then I'll go and sulk until tomorrow."

Too bad it don't happen that way. If she ain't in heat, she'll bite me and kick my butt from here to kingdom come. That's kinda nice for someone who's *getting it* on a semi-never basis, don't you think?

Detective Rodriguez at your service . . . that's me. I get paid for my services but I don't get to do the servicing.

I'm a Maytag washing machine repairhorse. I'm the loneliest horse in the world! I wait for the phone to ring – it never does. And if it did it wouldn't be the Best Western Hotel. It would be at "Best" a wrong number.

I'm the jester up against *The Jack* on the throne. I write the speech; King Studdly presents the *speech from the throne* (service) and convinces everyone in the kingdom that he is magnificent, that it was miraculous, divine, immaculate – and truly a religious experience. Poppycock! it's just not fair.

I'm going to find me a new profession. One that grants me a few of the blessings of life. Don't get me wrong. I'll be careful. I don't want to necessarily be a sleaze but I sure don't want to be a tease anymore!!

Well, I've said my *piece* . . . now I'm gonna go out there and get me some! Oh yeeeeah!!

Parlez-vous Texan?

You can order it by the fancy European name
if you want to...But Big Marnie® is all the French
you'll ever need to know in Texas.

Prince Charles Explains:
How To Fall Off A Horse Properly

Falling Off A Horse Properly is not only the game that has *all* of England talking, but it's the most original sport invented by a Royal since King Charles I created the very popular, *Throw The Peasant In The Moat* (unofficially known as: Drop The Subject Before The Subject Drops You!).

The man, ~~who will be king, who should, who will most likely be, quite possibly be~~, who'll perhaps someday be king, ~~(If his mother would only take a hint)~~ discusses the finer points of Intentional Spontaneous Dismount. He calls it temporarily free falling in nature – an alternative to merely sitting tall in the saddle. His unorthodox style, once it catches on, will no doubt be copied by riders around the world. His initiative is perhaps the first and most cleverly *mounted* by a member of the Royal Family to salvage the ailing monarchy.

This brief plunge into the world of vacating the saddle region by HRH (His Royal ~~Highness~~ Harness) Prince Charles, will be immediately followed by an official apology from Buckingham Palace to all British subjects, for Charles' apparent lack of ~~common~~ Royal Sense by appearing in *such a shoddy* publication as Penthorse. This will, in turn, be followed by an unofficial apology by Penthorse Magazine to Charles himself, for ruffling The Royal Family's feathers – and getting the Bonnie Prince into hot water.

From The Throne To The Loam

I must level with you somewhat here. I come from a rather privileged family background. It has been a great system for us for hundreds of years. However, the economic squeeze of the late twentieth century has taken its toll on everyone. The Royal family is constantly under the critical eyes of both the media and the public. Each year our $14,000,000 allowance to run the palace comes under review. In recent years, or since I developed my new riding style, I've found that it's hard for the public purse to say no to a prince with his arm in a sling or his leg in a cast.

First off, I would like to make one thing perfectly clear. The old maxim that learning to ride a horse is as easy as falling off a horse is a lot of horsebuns. Riding a horse is one thing, falling off a horse "properly", is quite another. Of course by "properly" we are at once commonly and royally referring to I.S.D. (Intentional Spontaneous Dismount) At first glance it would appear that one is merely dethroned – perhaps even taken quite by surprise. But closer study reveals that this is indeed an art.

Any fool can take a tumble and jump back up and say, "I'm okay". I say, give the people their money's worth and they'll not only come back to the event next year to watch you do it again, but, "God willing", they'll dig a little deeper into their already shallow pockets and we get to be top dog for a wee while longer.

It just makes good business sense to ensure that spectators leave an event feeling like they came and saw what they came to see.

Take professional wrestling for instance. Sure, there's some faking involved, but it certainly pays the bills doesn't it?

Recognising the horse and it's parts.
The Horse (parts)
(Head, ears (for verbal commands), neck and mane, back (saddle goes here), tail, posterior (avoid this area), front legs and feet (avoid getting under feet), back legs and feet (avoid back feet), belly, naughty bits - avoid unless you want to be walloped to death.

Horses are quadrupeds (having four legs). Except for Quarter Horses, who only have one if they are divvied up one leg per quarter (it would be like riding a pogo stick). Or sometimes they have none, if they are quartered end to end and you are unfortunate enough to get one of the two middle quarter sections. If you are thinking of falling off a Quarter Horse, strive to own one with at least one leg. While more awkward at first than some of the other breeds, you'll get on to it.

If you speak English, an English riding horse is ideal. If you don't, find one that understands your native tongue or, at the very least, your incoherent commands.

The Rider Does Not Act Alone

The rider and horse must be one. This is perhaps the single most important aspect of this new sport. You must be prepared to devote the time for the extensive training involved here, otherwise you could end up having "an accident" and real injury can occur. Let's avoid internal bleeding at all cost, shall we? After all, the idea is not to actually kill yourself, but to gain continuing support, minor attention, varying degrees of sympathy or personal pleasure – when you simply want to create a complete spectacle of yourself.

Everyone will develop their favorite ways of signalling their horse.

Perhaps it will be a series of foot nudges, rein jerks – or perhaps maybe you'll favour incoherent verbal commands. (At least incoherent to your fellow horsemen and to on-lookers.)

Taking The Safe Plunge – Some Win-Fall Tips

*Don't ever attempt anything too dangerous. Always make them think that it was an accident though. They must not suspect in the least that it was intentional. If you're caught faking you will risk being disqualified from the event or exiled.

*If you wish to discredit another rider, do so at your own leisure, but *do* make it appear as though you were pushed. Spectators and members of the press love an uproar centered around foul play. Unsportsmanlike conduct on the part of your opponent makes for good headlines in the newspapers.

*Always pretend you're hurt and that you need to be taken to a hospital. This way you not only accumulate the greatest amount of sympathy points but you miss the rest of a no doubt dangerous event – avoiding serious injury *and* you get to go for a nice ambulance ride as well.

*Bottomline! Always get in the newspaper! Always get on television!

Some Of My Favorite Mishaps are:

Going For The Big Loop – This involves groin injury, excessive amounts of moaning and groaning and rolling about on the ground, holding the family jewels region of the anatomy. There is always some question as to whether or not there will be any more heirs to the throne. It's a spectator favorite.

The Nose Dive – This one involves full gallop, a rather large embankment and near drowning. One uses the stirrups to catapult oneself forward into a mud pit or septic trench. You must remember to hold your breath on this one or the threat of drowning could become a reality. Her Majesty's Royal Mounted Ninny Physicians are usually called in on this one – bearing hot towels and a rude tasting beverage. A stretcher will be necessary to remove you from the field.

Being Dragged A Great Distance By One Leg – Being dragged, quite intentionally, for approximately 2.5 kilometres is somewhat more dangerous. However, one leg is safely caught in the stirrup the other flaps and flails about with the rest of your body until the horse comes to a halt at a predetermined position. At this point, you merely, but dramatically, fall to the ground breaking your fall with your arms like Hulk Hogan. The helmet, of course, is key in this exercise, as are well developed stomach muscles to keep your entire body from actually bouncing along the roadway.

Being thrown into Lady Chatterley's Rather Walloping Large Bosom Quite By Accident And Breaking One's Nose – Well, I think this one is pretty self-explanatory. Break falls aren't going to prepare you for this highly controversial type of landing. It is not something you can fake or escape. If it does occur, as it has to me – only once thank God!, it will be months before you can comfortably blow your nose again and years before you can actually face Lady Chatterley without dancing and dodging about her like a boxer anticipating a left hook. You may never escape the fear that it could quite possibly happen twice in a lifetime.

After any one of these mishaps, a nice long outing on the Royal Yacht Britannia is quite in order.

Lots Of Other Jolly Good Tricks

There are many other ways of leaving the saddle, ending up on the ground and not injuring yourself. No doubt you'll want to invent some of your own. Remember, World Wrestling Federation should be viewed on a weekly basis to pick up safety techniques not found in riding books.

I visualise a day when Falling Off A Horse really becomes a serious sport, other than merely using it for guaranteeing one's annual allowance.

I see a sport where the ultimate objective and challenge (not to mention point winner) will be for the competitor to convince the spectators that he has in fact been killed. The trick here is, living to tell. To come back next year – amidst rumors of your death – and do it to them all over again. That's my idea of a champion, a professional and a Royal Horseman.

One final note:

I just noticed this rather ominous poetry excerpt from the Highwayman. I see that the words "Tim the Osler" are doubly underlined. As a horseman, I've come across many stable hands in my career most of them jolly good, but a few were psychos – I fear Tim is a member of the latter group. To any horse who is reading this, I strongly suggest you distance yourself from this, this . . . "Tim the Osler (as far as you are able from that stable).

THE HIGHWAYMAN QUOTE

"Deep in the dark old Inn yard
A stable wicket creaked
Where "Tim the Osler" listened
His face was white and peaked
His eyes were hollows of madness
His hair like mouldy hay
Dumb as a dog he listened
And heard the robber say
One kiss my Bonnie sweetheart
I'm after my prize tonight
But I shall be back with the yellow gold
Before the morning light
But if they press me sharply
And hurry me through the day
Then look for me by moonlight
Watch for me by moonlight
I'll come to thee by moonlight
Though Hell shall bar the way"

About Prince Charles:
Prince Charles is the future King of England, a horseman, a jet pilot and the author of a soon-to-be-released book on the difficulties of surviving a fairy tale marriage entitled: *Never Say Di!*

REAMS *of* DIVERSIONS

AREN'T HUMANS SMART?

Human intelligence is apparently not yet available to everyone. It appears that a large portion of the tablet – swallowing public must be warned not to mistake the tiny (by comparison) medication for a very large grey and yellow cannister boldly marked, DO NOT EAT!!! Their function is to absorb moisture in pill bottles and aren't to be used as food.

Many of the victims hospitalized after ingesting the big plastic wads have come directly from being contestants on the very popular game show: *Spot The Brain Cell.*

And *we* get into a barrel of oats and who ends up getting called stupid? Hmmm?

If libel suits are responsible for the above-rump covering, then they can keep their sophistication and we'll keep pretending we're as dense as fence posts and everyone will be much happier.

MR. ED STILL ALIVE AND KICKING

According to his publicity agent, Mr. Ed, of television bitcom fame, is still well and very much unattached. Through an interpreter, he told Penthorse that, "I'm still looking, still talking – when nobody's around –

and will whisper sweet nothings until dawn in the right candidate's ears...as long as they promise not to tell Wilbur!"
It's hard to keep a good horse down.

TITHEAD PAINTING HEISTED

It has been described as the largest art heist in recent mammary. The owners of the masterpiece are extremely upset, as the coveted Tithead painting is perhaps the most realistic and honest representation of

twentieth-century man. No doubt somebody will be milking somebody for a huge ransom.

Rumor has it that the thieves have been offered $4,000,000. Rumor also has it that they'll probably try squeezing for a lot more.

The work of art was originally considerably smaller. It then became the first painting in history to undergo a silicone-to-canvas implant, thus enlarging its dimensions as well as its value as a

hostage. It was a first for both medical and art history.

PEOPLE CHASE BECOMING MORE POPULAR

People-chase has become all the rage. The sport entails releasing droves of humans onto a pre-determined course. Horses will then chase the humans until the latter froth at the mouth and give up. The horse who accumulates the largest number of people in the two-hour event is declared the winner.

14

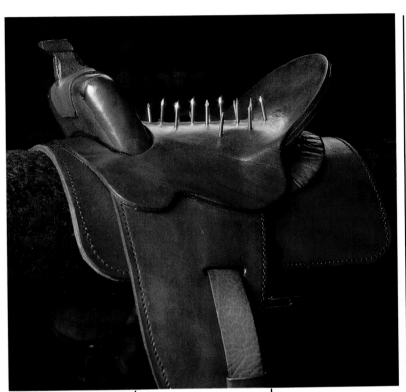

SADDLE MASOCHISM

Is this seat taken?
A company in Butte, Montana, is manufacturing a new saddle that's really catching on in the big urban centers – as a home entertainment center *and* as a love accessory.

This innovative new product has also made horseback riding more popular than *ever* among the "hurt me, beat me, love me" groups.

"Like many things, it's a pain in the butt when you first start off, but shortly thereafter it feels really great!", exclaimed a delighted saddle owner.

A spokesman for the *Yeeeooow Saddle Company Inc.,* says they've been back-ordered for six months. "It's funny how we can be doing so well when our business in general is *'really hurting'.*"

THE WORLD'S FIRST PEDIGREE

A diagram of a 5000-year-old pedigree has been found in Persia. It is carved on the surface of a stone among artifacts known to have been used by man around 3000 B.C. The horses with upright manes represent wild stallions, hanging manes domesticated stallions, and those without manes are mares. The illustration is believed to be the first pedigree.

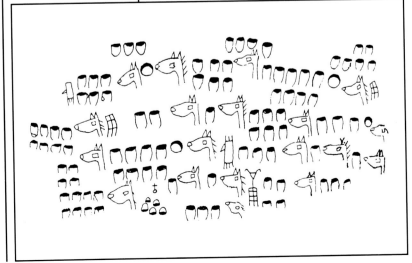

SOCIAL SECURITY

With so many social diseases out there to choose from, it makes it difficult to decide which one, when and with whom.

It's also astounding to discover that many young horses these days are ignoring the facts about Sexually Transmitted Diseases (STD). Yet, this is exactly what the surveys are revealing.

The reasons? They either think that it can't happen to them OR perhaps they aren't sure what a condom looks like.

So, for the record: It can happen to you! And for the naive group- and the timid ones; this is what a Trojan Horse™ condom looks like up close.

Ignorance is never an excuse. Take charge! It's clearly a matter of life and death.

Shown slightly smaller than actual size.

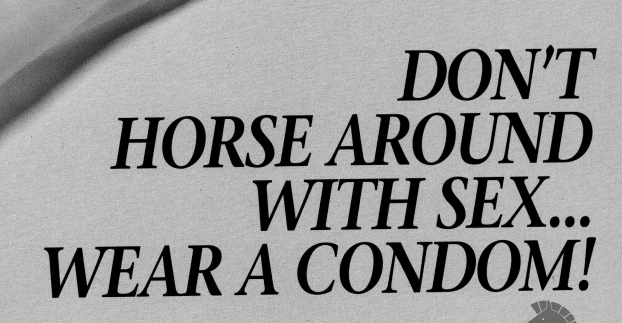

DON'T
HORSE AROUND
WITH SEX...
WEAR A CONDOM!

TROJAN-HORSE®

The Rise and Demise of Rock Star ★★★ SPIKE SPURR

Between Rock and a Horrid Place!

The bizarre world of rock star Spike Spurr has changed. It used to be, when Spike grabbed the mike the whole world was watching . . . watching . . . watching . . . they kept watching to see where those big clumsy feet of his were going to step next.

He comes from Liverpool, home of the legendary group. "The Buckles": John, Paul, George and Gringo. Even *they* thought Spike's career would never end. Of Spurr's talent, Gringo Scarr remarks: "We All Lived In A Yellow Tub Of Cream, A Yellow Tub Of Cream, A Yellow Tub Of Cream, We All Lived In A Yellow Tub Of Cream . . . but Spike . . . Spike was the whole damn cow. The udder from the gutter. He took the beat from the street and turned it into heat. He was the real cream who rose to the top, only to sour and curdle while the world watched him drown in sea of humiliation. Humiliation inflicted by his record company. It's a shame we never signed him to our label. Someone else got there first".

Two years ago Spike Spurr was on top of the charts, and if there was any truth to the rumours in the tabloids, that's not the only thing he was on top of. Spike had a *huge* following of groupies.

He was Radical, Rich and Raunchy. (His own version of the 3 R's). He didn't *Read* much, he was always *Right* anyway, and *Rithmetic* went out the window with his formal education.

Today, he's Depressed, Dejected and Desperate. The 3 D's have not been kind to Spike. Yet his talent went from 3-D to barely 1-D, seemingly overnight.

For this, Spike blames his record company and is presently suing Prairie Prune Records for a record one hundred trillion dollars.

We don't blame him a bit. His Rock/Punk/New Wave/Alternative, hit album **"SHOCK THE DONKEY"** soared to Number One quicker than his fans' parents could say: "You're not listening to that heathen music of Spike Spurr in this barn!!!"

Spike was flying high. But his good fortune would soon change as a result of incredible pressure, applied by Prairie Prune record executives, to cash in on what was an industry prediction that a Recreation Room Dance Craze (The Barn Dance) was making a comeback. Because of economic hard times, fans would stop going out and begin focusing on a more stable arrangement – staying in – and making their own fun like they did in the old days.

What ensued was Spike's Big Bomb, the party favorites album, **"Where's The Party??"** It didn't work.

This album sits at 251 on the charts, but the chart only goes to 250. Once again, Spike outdoes even himself. By comparison, sitting at 151 on the charts is the en-vironmentalist offering "Whale Music – The Sounds Of The Humpback Whale: Their Music, Their Language, Their Politics".

Spike's career has about as much chance of survival as the whales. It will take a miracle.

Note the difference in the lyrics. Compare the incredible depth of his political activist/social comment album "Shock The Donkey", to the shallow lyrics of, **"Where's The Party???"** (His Boneheads' **"Acting Stupid"** album).

Shock The Donkey
words and music by
Spike Spurr
Prairie Prune Records

They're livin' up in their cozy white cages,
They're suckin' our blood out,
 our blood out in stages,
It's a storybook life and they
 tear out our pages,
We're taxed to death and
 we ain't got no wages.

They've gone a bit Wonkey
They'll drive us all Bonkey
If we don't Shock The Donkey!

We Must!
(Everyone Sing)

Shock The Donkey, drive it Wonkey
Everyone Shock The Don-key
Shock The Donkey Bongo Bonkey
Everyone Shock The Don-key
Everyone Shock Everyone Shock
Everyone Shock Everyone Shock

(Repeat until it seems
like the song should be over) (Then Fade)

©1989 Spike Spurr

Where's The Party???
words and music by
Spike Spurr
Prairie Prune Records

Has anyone seen the party?
Does anyone want to go?
Has anyone thrown a jockey?
Does anyone want to, though?

Does everyone want to party?
Has anyone answered NO!?
Can anyone get a car?
Does everyone want to blow?

Has anyone seen the party?
Does anyone want to strut?
Does anyone own a trailer?
Does anyone own a truck?

I said does anyone own a Trailer?
I said does anyone own a truck?
I said has anyone seen a party?
I said does anyone want to BUCK?

Wanna Buck? Wanna Buck?
Buck! Buck! Buck!
Party! Party! Party!
(Fade! Fade! Fade!)

©1991 Spike Spurr

Spike Update!!!!!
For immediate release!!!!!!

From Demise to Surprise – Miracles Do Happen
There has been a last-minute break-through in Spike Spurr's career! This news bulletin and press release was handed to us just moments ago. About the only thing that can save Spike's career and his relationship with his record company is this compromise:

Prairie Prune Acknowledges that their prediction was wrong (In a phrase: Spit Happens!!) The damages suit will still continue and there **will** be a fair settlement somewhere down the road, the outcome to be decided by the courts.

Spike will release, immediately, what he and everyone else hopes will be a career-salvaging record. It will be Spike's first Wrap Album. Wrap is something the record company **knows** is popular; they just aren't quite sure why yet. Neither is anybody else. It may very well remain a mystery for ever.

The album is called: **Spike Spurr's Wrap Album** and includes the hit single, **Sprain My Leg Baby!**

Sprain My Leg Baby is not a hit yet, but the confidence is right there on the front of the cover. If this reflects the new commitment, marketing philosophy and optimism on the part of Prairie Prune Records, then maybe, just maybe, once again, Spike Spurr has a chance to catapult to the top of the charts as he did so effortlessly such a short time ago.

Alive with smoke!

We've taken away the tar. We've stripped away the nicotine and left the bare essential - smoke! After all, if smoke isn't what smoking's all about, why would they call it "smoking"?

Nudeport

Nudeport

MENTHOL BOX

THE SURGEON GENERAL'S LITTLE COMMENT BOX:
Careless smoking has been known to cause: barn fires, more barn fires, and the very tragic - often resulting in great loss of life - Barn Fire! (Step on it! Spit on it! Somebody put that thing out. What are you trying to do, start a Barn Fire???)

Low on tar. Big on smoke.
0 mg. tar 0 mg. nicotine
100% smoke

© Nudeport Tobacco Inc.

Why The Long Face?

Breeding Horses To Win By A Nose.

More and more athletes are choosing substance-abuse as a means of coping with fame and mega-multi-million dollar sports deals. Steroid use is running rampant in Olympic sport for several reasons: It's partly for the glory of winning but it's mostly for the lucrative endorsements which await gold medal winners.

You can't help but wonder if money hasn't already ruined amateur *and* professional sports.

It appears that, until now, the only sport left with any integrity is professional Horse Racing...but perhaps that will all change soon, too.

Science, Opportunity and Greed – Together Again

Why is it whenever Opportunity rents the bottom half of a house, Greed always moves in upstairs.

Then one night Greed has Opportunity up for dinner. A golden "opportunity" to meet the neighbors.

When Common Sense drops in by accident, Greed then pops a little something in Common Sense's drinkie and next thing you know, over the balcony goes Common Sense and that's the end of that.

Now with Common Sense permanently out of the picture – wouldn't ya know it – the two of them end up exchanging new ideas, comparing notes and scheming schemes that have never been schemed quite like this before.

Greed opens up by saying: "It schemes to me that the difference between winning and losing often boils down to a few inches. Like they say up in Jersey, after reviewing several thousand photo-finishes, Da-nose that crosses Da-finish line before Da-rest... Da-wins! – and that's all she wrote! There ain't no second chances!"

Opportunity "dittoed" that one and added: "It schemes to me that if winning *does* in fact come down to inches, that whoever had an advantage, of say, oh, a few extra inches in front – perhaps a few extra inches of "nose" – would, over time, win more races, which in turn would translate into making more money!!! Maybe it's possible to lengthen the Schnoz?"

Greed agreed with Opportunity's comments and added: "I have a geneticist friend up in New Jersey whose been toying around with some interesting experiments. Sticking his nose where God might not want him to have it. He's realizing amazing success. Maybe we ought to give him a call..."

Well, they did...*And* a remarkable series of events are rumored to be evolving which might make one ask oneself "Is greed the mother of invention or a 'mother' of an invention?"

Will Genetic Manipulation Change the Face of Horse Racing?

Is This Kind of Genetic Engineering Possible?

Anything's possible. Some say that medical miracles of this nature aren't achievable just yet. But there are others who insist it's here and it's happening. Still others say that there are some very convincing satellite photos of unusual-looking horses and of nude beaches, to back it up. One such person is a doctor who's name we aren't about to mention for very obvious reasons.

This is one respected German geneticist's explanation of how it could all be true. (Dr. Gene Krommelzonal has asked that his identity not be made known so his life will not be endangered. We would like to thank Dr. Krommelzonal for *not* (I repeat, NOT!!) sharing his expertise in the area of genetics. Thanks again, Gene! You were a great help in *not* getting this article written.)

(To be spoken with a light German accent)

As a familiar unknown scientist in zee area of genetics I will say it is a known fact that nose-size is a highly heritable trait. So if one culls out all offspring born with average-size noses and keeps for breeding purposes only those horses with noses ranging from big, all the way up to huge and comically large, this alone would make an incredible difference over several generations. But generations take a long time – to be specific – they often take several generations. So even though selective breeding would be one way of achieving larger results, it will not be the sole process used to lengthen the nose.

Very Advanced Genetic Engineering

This probably sounds far-fetched, but what if it were possible to remove the gene responsible for determining the anteater's nose size and then using very Advanced Gene Insertion Techniques (Micro-Eentzee-Weenzee Surgery) they are placed into a mare's unfertilized eggs.

They must first find the nose gene and switch it with zee Big Nose Gene. They will be replacing the normal existing genes which determine a much shorter, average-sized nose.

If the pioneers of this brand of surgery are able to do this right now, it would save them several million years of the evolutionary process – a powerful lot of standing around – and would allow somebody to reap profits *immediately*. Profits which would be much larger than the noses themselves.

So if they use Advanced Gene Insertion Techniques at the egg stage to switch the genes and replace nice, normal-sized nose genes with overtly bizarre, humungous and laughable nose size genes, it *could* work.

Then, in the lab, they fertilize the eggs in a test tube and wait until the eggs are more developed. Then, by utilizing the already widely-practised embryo transplants, they could, in a very short space of time have a great number of long-nosed horses being born to dozens of host mares. Within two years, they could be not only up and running but quite capable of pulling off a win shortly after rounding the club house turn. This is at once amazing and frightening.

Q. & A.

Q. Will a mare bearing a foal that has a nose with size 16 nostrils be able to give birth without major risk either to her or the foal?
A. As long as the foal comes out nose first everything should come off without a hitch. However, if the head and nose get turned around inside the mare the risks of losing both the mare and the foal increase.
Q. What happens when they get a head cold?
A. You've got a big problem on your hands. It's conceivable that half their body could be under seige. Not to mention the monotony of carrying away buckets and buckets of snot.
Q. What happens when their nose starts running, too? Do they blow the race if they have to stop to blow their noses?
A. Well, if their nose starts running by itself that's another can of worms. But since 90% of the pop-

ulation wouldn't believe this conversation anyway, I can't rule out the possibility that a nose could win a race – on its own, without the horse – but it would have to be able to run very, very fast.
Q. Sure they'll win races but will they still be able to hold their heads up?
A. From a pride standpoint, it's doubtful. From a size-and-weight standpoint, depending on the degree of mutation, it could range from sure/maybe, to a prop-it-up-with-a-stick-impossibility. Somebody should be having grave concerns about the serious problems it will no doubt create down the line.
Q. Will the nose's length develop to the point where the race is over before it even starts?
A. Perhaps, but that's unlikely. It would be an exceedingly long nose, indeed, in order for that to happen.

The Evolution Of The Human Race

The stages in man's development from a blithering apelike ancestor to a thoroughly modern human being are shown below:

PLIOPITHICUS
A protoape to the gibbon. Did resemble some modern politicians.

AUSTRALOPITHICUS AFRICANUS
Probably a descendant of something earlier – walked upright on two legs and picked his nose and butt a lot. Did not think of the future!

NEANDERTHAL MAN
Was not a brute as many people think. Skull capacity bigger than many modern humans. Made tools and was hairy like the greeks.

CRO-MAGNON MAN
Replaced Neanderthal man in Europe left the world cave paintings and carvings that are now famous (typically after he's dead!) never received a red cent for them.

MODERN MAN
Physically much like Cro-Magnon. Grew food, domesticated animals, attacked neighboring countries, pre-occupied with sex.

TIT-HEAD MODERNICUS
Twentieth Century Man or Six Million Dollar Man. Food comes from store. Exploit anything that moves. Worry about feelings later or never.

It is at the Tit-Head stage where gene manipulation takes place. Greed replaces common sense on evolutionary scale.

The Evolution Of Winning Races

EOHIPPUS
Extremely stand-off-ish. Nibbled a bit, then swallowed.

MESOHIPPUS
Very stand-off-ish. Nibbled more, then swallowed.

PARAHIPPUS
Stand-off-ish. Nibbled, chewed, then swallowed.

EQUUS
Trusting, vulnerable, likes sugar cubes and carrots.

BIG NOSE
Head heavy, likes to run like hell.

Who's The Geneticist? Who Has the Formula?

It's rumored that by next spring Nosy Acres Farms, owned and operated by the powerful Gambenosie Mafia Family will be running one such genetic freak in the Derby. If it happens to win, it's going to put more than one nose out of joint and it probably won't belong to the winner.

The Gambenosie Family are the ones sinking all the cash into the project. If it works, they are the ones who will be raking in the loot over the next few years. They will be almost impossible to beat.

As far as the geneticist goes?...Nobody knows for sure. His identity will be kept very secret. The security around him impossible to penetrate. It would be safe to say that he's extremely bright. And if you're a gambler, you can bet that right now he could probably write his own ticket to anywhere...he just might not make it to the plane without getting blowed-up-reeeal-goood!

Advanced Scientific Breakthrough or Human Stupidity?

The problem with humans is that they can't stand to be out-done. So if somebody invents a formula to improve their odds of winning and it works, it isn't long before everybody else is doing the same thing to improve their own chances. It takes a lot of losers for any one person to win a major event. It only takes one loser (and a lot of followers) to start a trend that can lead an entire industry down the road to ruin. To each and every truth there are many consequences. We can only hope that whoever is involved here has weighed them all carefully.

Schnozzmedic Surgery – Alternative to Gene Manipulation

Without the formula, there will be little that others can do besides selective breeding and enlargement through the little-proven Schnozzmedic Surgery. This kind of surgery is fine when one is reducing the size of the nose. But when you are enlarging the nose, it requires bone and hide grafts, hair replacement and the least accessible – a donor!! The surgery must be so expertly done that it cannot be detected by veterinarians or racing officials. If it is detected, the horse is dis-qualified and permanently sus-pended from racing. In fact Schnozzmedic Surgery is illegal, whereas the genetic mutants may not be.

At the very least, it will be extremely interesting to see how this story unfolds. As far as the outcome goes "Who Nose?!?"...I guess we're all just going to have to wait and see.

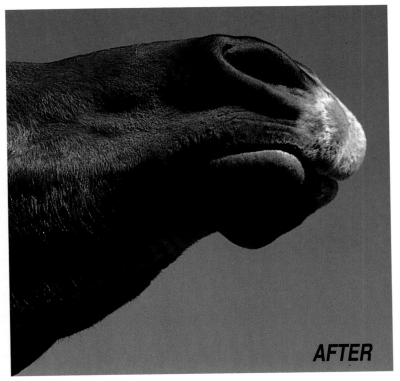

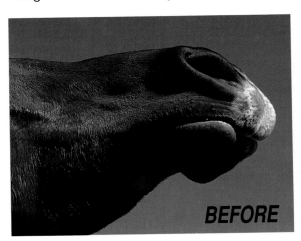

BEFORE

AFTER

Random Horse Book Club®

C.I. Agent's, *When Dead Men Wheeze,* the exciting sequel to *Was Oswald Asthmatic?*
Oh no! Not the Kennedy thing again!

Yes, it is the Kennedy thing again and I don't want to hear another peep out of you! Before you start running off at the mouth about beating a dead horse . . . How can you be so sure that J.F.K. isn't a vegetable somewhere? How can you doubt the possibility that he and Oswald were in cahoots from the very beginning? How do we know they didn't have a "thing" for each other and were just trying to get rid of Jackie and ah . . . Jackie and ah . . . ah . . . Olga! . . . Yeah, that's her name . . . Olga! (Yes, the Russian peasant girl, the one the gypsy fortune teller said would bring fame, shame and blame probably leading to death [or at the very least, disappearance] to any man who was foolish enough to marry her. Well, Oswald walked into that one didn't he?)

What do you have to say about the rumour pointing to suspicious sounding evidence that the blood stains on the open limo were ketchup and chicken gravy, huh?? What do you have to say now, big mouth?!? Maybe Oswald's still alive and maybe he isn't and maybe that's what this book's about, horse-lips! So why don't you stop being so cheap and cough up one penny and buy it!

Author *C.I. Agent's* moving, investigative fabrication based on a fascinating series of original rumours, is breath taking. **– Daily News –**

Was it Oswald he heard wheezing *that* night on *that* rooftop just two years ago from this *very* day? Find out for just one exciting, breath taking, penny!!!! **– Random Horse Book Club**

(Any excess profits from, C.I. Agent's, exciting, strange and most likely really true new book will be donated to the Oswald Survivors' Fund – "On the flee since '63".)

The Importance of Being Harnessed
A Random Horse Classic By Oscar Wildhorse

This unrestrained humor classic by Oscar Wildhorse is perhaps the funniest (and only) explanation as to "why" in any language. You'll be geared up from the moment you open the book. Chapter after chapter of side-splitting laughter and hints on how you, too, can be a delinquent runaway horse, making each day a memorable one for our excitable two-legged friends.

Kill yourself laughing (and anyone on board) with such hysterical chapters as:
1) "Hey! Let's Run in the Ditch for Awhile."
2) "Last One over the Thirty Foot Embankment is a Rotten Egg!"
3) "Watch the Bough! Watch the Tree! Watch the Bough! . . . Bonk!! Ooops! . . . Sorry!"
It's Oscar Wildhorse at his out of control, trouble-making best.

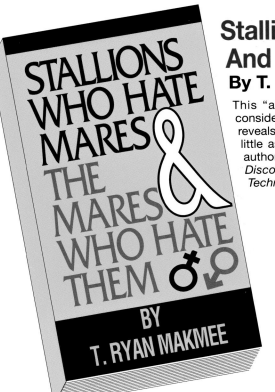

Stallions Who Hate Mares And The Mares Who Hate Them
By T. Ryan Makmee

This "all about hate" book is geared for the Hate Lover or anyone who is considering giving up on love and starting to hate as an interesting alternative. It reveals, in no uncertain terms, that it's just as dangerous for horses to hate too little as it is for them to love too much. All in all, a very interesting read by the author of: *"I Said, I Told You To Shut Up First!!!" – A Novice's Guide To Marital Discord* and *"I Don't Care If The Neighbors Can Hear Us, Audrey!!!"* (Arguing Techniques For Apartment Dwellers).

How To Make A Million Bucks In The Bale Order Business
By Meg A. Kash

Selling hay and straw through the mail can make you rich fast – especially in the drought years. Just ask author Meg A. Kash. She made over ten million dollars by paying nothing and selling high-volume through bale/mail order. Even if you don't have any money, storage facilities, or even hay and straw of your own, Meg shows you how to sell – for big profits – the stuff that's around the corner from your stall. Right out from under their noses . . . (Nudge! Nudge! Wink! Wink!)!

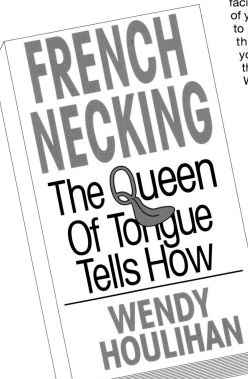

From the cover girl of Penthorse comes an exciting and romantic new release . . .
French Necking – The Queen Of Tongue Tells How

Author, Wendy (Wet Lips) Houlihan tells her secrets once and for all in this illustrated encyclopedia of tongue-ology. Explicit photography shows you how to do it all. From sneaking up on the candidate (victim) through tickling their fancy *and* their esophagus *and* how to turn a chance meeting with fate and saliva into a follow-up date where the fun begins all over again. That's right, now you'll be able to turn even the shyest of victims (candidates) into Plunge-O-Smootch-O-Maniacs. *And* you'll be mastering the technique that has won for the author the hearts of dozens, the admiration of hundreds, the mouths and throats of thousands and the million dollar monicker: "Wet Lips Houlihan".
Why wait for spring? Do it now!

BY R.U.CUMMINGS

"I'll meet you half-way...I'll come over if you come across"

FENCES & HEDGES

FENCES & HEDGES

20 CLASS A CIGARETTES

WARNING: Her Majesty's Royal Mounted Ninny Physicians have deemed that cigarette-smoking is a raaather ghastly habit for one to indulge oneself in before, after or during a competition. It not only impedes one's ability to properly inhale oxygen, but it sours one's breath and makes social intercourse a tedious and unpleasant task for the non-smoking horse. So there you have it - straight from the horse's mouth!

SPRINT EASTWOOD as FILTHY HARRY in
MAGNUM
HORSE II
GO AHEAD, MAKE MY HAY!
OPENING JUNE 1

MOVIES & VIDEO

THE Ex-HORSE-IST III IT'S ME AGAIN!

The Ex-Horse-ist III It's Me Again!

Something is happening to a horse, in a room in a barn, on *this* street. A man has been called to make it go away . . . again! He is the Ex-Horse-ist.

This is not the first time he's been to this address. It is not the second time. It's the third time. And judging by the ending of part three, I suspect it is not the last time.

There was some comic relief (not that it was at all scary) when

The Ex-Horse-ist (Bertrand Strange) said to the demonic foal: "If we don't co-operate this time we'll be putting that crucifix where there ain't no light and leaving it there".

Well, you should have seen what followed.

Although there were few surprises, there were some additions. The possessed (played by Linda Brooder's real life younger sister) managed to make not only the crucifix disappear but also numerous other items, e.g., some small

appliances including a toaster-oven with upper and lower elements allowing you the flexibility to toast both sides of the slice at once. This film is not for the squeamish. (If the film bombs she could certainly take *that* show on the road and draw sell-out crowds on the bar circuit around the country.) I had heard a rumour that the **JiffyStor®** self-storage company was after her for an endorsement. Their present advertising slogan is: **"JiffyStor® . . . What I can't fit in here ain't worth ownin'!"**

Although the Ex-Horse-ist de-demonizing chants were charming I honestly think they were useless against Lucifer's henchmen. They might merely come out temporarily, just to see what kind of a bozo was running off at the mouth. But seriously folks, this kind of unprofessional exorcising is not only dangerous, but leaves the door wide open for demonic repossession (The Sequel).

Note the following pathetic chants:

Pathetic Chant #1
*Bog spavin, bone spavin,
   thoroughpin curb
Over in the knee in the
   meadow in the herd
Cribbing, Nibbling, Shoe
   boil hive
Over in the meadow
   eatin' horse fly pie.*

Pathetic Chant #2
*Yicka Yack Swayback
Fracka Flicka Foal
Come Back Devil's
   Snack
Devil's Up a Pole*

*Jibber Jab Devil's Bad
Demon's on the run
Run Away all day
I saw your bare bum*

I don't know about you but if I were a demon the above certainly wouldn't scare the bejesus out of me. Which leads me to suspect they are not trying to rid her of the devil . . . just yet. This will more than likely result in another horrid sequel.

* * *

The Veterinarian Always Rings Twice

With Friends Like This Who Needs Enemas?

You can bet nobody said, "Break a leg opening night", on this baby.

Bring along a horse blanket. This is thriller-chiller from start to finish.

Let me tell you, for a small black bag it sure is filled to the brim with dirty tricks. And watch out for that damned rubber glove! Don't forget what the Oxford English Dictionary says about the word enema: It is a noun. Whew! Thank God for that.

However, cancel the caterers and the balloons "cause it's all downhill from here . . . Ah . . . Once again, the Concise Oxford definition of the word enema:
enema n. Injection of liquid or gas into rectum especially to expel its contents. A fluid or syringe is used. (As you can well see, it's not exactly like knocking off a candy store. Then it goes on and makes some reference to the Greeks . . . which does not surprise me if you catch my drift.) Mind you, this is routine Vet visit stuff which is hammered home to scare the living dickens out of even horses of sound confirmation and

stable health. Believe me, it's real!

Make sure you don't leave your seat. If you're planning to have popcorn, get it on the way in – because you don't want to leave your seat uncovered.

It's a must-see if you're into suspense or having the %#!@ (Dickens) scared out of you.

This is the movie version of the Broadway production from the makers of the Summer Hit of 1990: **The Vegetarian Always Brings Rice** *With Friends Like This Who Needs Endive?*

★ ★ ★

Magnum Horse 2 Starring Sprint Eastwood as Filthy Harry

This is Sprint Eastwood and Filthy Harry at their absolute best. I don't want to spoil the film for you but this is exactly what

happens.

Go Ahead, Make My Hay!

It really boils down to Filthy Harry meets the Lazy Farmer. You see, the lazy farmer decided that Haying Time was not his favorite time of the year because it's always a hundred degrees out and the humidity is unbearable. It can be just above freezing the day before Haying Time and as soon as you pull the baler out of the implement shed, as soon as the nose of the tractor creeps past the sliding door, you'll hear this big **BOING!!!!!!** and it is instantly a hundred degrees out!

So, the Lazy Farmer decided that he wasn't going to make hay this year when the sun was shining or even if wasn't. He was not going to do it this year or any other year from now on. The animals could bloody well eat something else. (Isn't it

funny . . . anyone who would want to make hay under typical haying conditions has got to out of his mind *or* at the very least crazy. But that's okay; we need more nuts running around. However, as soon as you don't want to make hay just once; you're a lazy slug, to your peers and what's even worse – to the livestock! It just isn't fair.)

Anyway, each animal would be given McDonalds "2 for 1 Value" coupons, an allowance, a public transportation pass. That should end the problems with **BOING!!!** This works fine and dandy until the livestock decides that McDonalds is not an acceptable substitute for a bale of hay. They hire Sprint Eastwood (Magnum Horse) and the drama unfolds.

Unfortunately, it was not going to work out well for Marvin Haymellow. Yesterday he was crazy just like everybody else. Today he is a lazy scoundrel who has the gall to classify himself as a farmer, and who is about to be taught a humungous lesson by the Filthiest Harry in the world.

Throughout the 90

minutes of action, Marvin Haymellow, former lunatic, turned Lazy Farmer (in the eyes of his peers, his steers and of course, every horse on the place) gets to suck on a .44 Magnum for about forty minutes of the film . . . ("Hey Marvin?! Either swallow it or spit the damn thing out!! But don't just sit there with it in your mouth.").

So then Filthy Harry blows every window out of the house, drags Marvin's butt out to the implement shed, throws him on the tractor, and says "Go ahead, make my hay!"

Well, Marvin may be crazy, but he's nobody's fool. So he cuts the hay, he rakes the hay, he bales the hay and then he puts the hay away. All the while he had a major gun to his head. I can't say I would have done things any differently.

When Filthy Harry leaves the premises, everything is as it should be. Tidy! Tidy! Tidy! The fields are bare, the barn is full, and everyone is thrilled except for Marvin. Mind you, he's looking forward to going back to being a full-time crazy and can hardly wait until next year's crop…I wonder why???

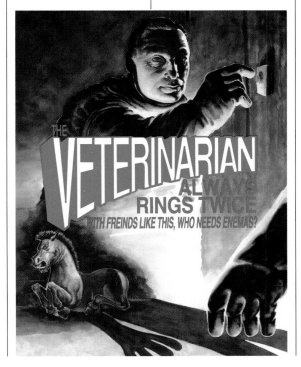

A Nightmare on Elm Street

PART IV
BACK FROM THE GLUE FACTORY

Night Mare On Elm Street Part IV

Freddie Glooger returns in:

Back from the Glue Factory

Looks like Freddie's back. Looks like Freddie's hacked. I guess the bus wasn't going to Reno after all. Gee, sorry about that Freddie! Thought we'd send you away on a holiday. No cost to Fred – don't have to pay. Give him swell accommodation (Send him to Hell and Damnation!). He wants a room with a view (He wants the room with

the Glue!).

Freddie's back and unforgiving, I doubt he'll leave a person living. He's here and there and in your dreams, he likes to hear your yells and screams. Freddie's back, he's here for more until he settles up the score. Freddie's back.

So you thought Freddie was spreading himself a little thin before! Had he not crawled out of the slicer in the *Nick* of time? Had he not swam to shore escaping meltdown in that vat of boiling glue?

Yes, Freddie would have been spreading himself exceedingly thin these days.

* * *

Freddie has a knack for coming back. It's hard to keep a good corpse down. If you liked the other three, it will be hard not to keep your eyes glued to the screen this time as Freddie comes back to stay.

In all the *Night Mare Films, Freddie has a way of sticking in your mind. This movie is no exception.*

– Playboar Magazine –

* * *

Even though Freddy's ugly as HELL and would most likely cut you to ribbons for taking more than five minutes to put on makeup, he'd probably make a really good husband if he had a lot of money. Plus he has that devilish personality and more power than Donald Trump and Merv Griffin put together.

– Cowsmopolitan Magazine –

33

How Old Do You Think I Am?

**Brush years off your looks with Equi-Fresh® Guaranteed!
If you don't look *and* feel younger within one day, we'll
give you your money back - and everyone elses, too.
How's *that* for an offer?**

**Equi-Fresh®, the dental formula from the
Anti-Aging and Fresh-Breath experts at
Oil Of Onay®.
Try it! You've nothing to lose but about
ten years!**

REGULAR FLAVOUR
FLUORIDE TOOTHPASTE

Equi-fresh

WHITER TEETH!
LOOK YOUNGER!
FRESH BREATH!

TRIPLE PROTECTION

150 mL

ANTI-AGING DENTAL FORMULA FROM
OIL OF ONAY

Miss Dusty Fields

Penthorse Center Foal of The Decade

"The only problem with being Center Foal quality material," 58-34-58 Dusty says, "is that a lot of horses - both male and female - assume you're stupid. I know what two buckets of oats plus two buckets of oats add up to...a big fat gut ache if you happen to eat them all at once!!! Ha! Ha! Ha!...See, when you're as good-looking as I am you have to have a sense of humor."

PENTHORSE CENTER FOAL
OF THE DECADE
Miss Dusty Fields

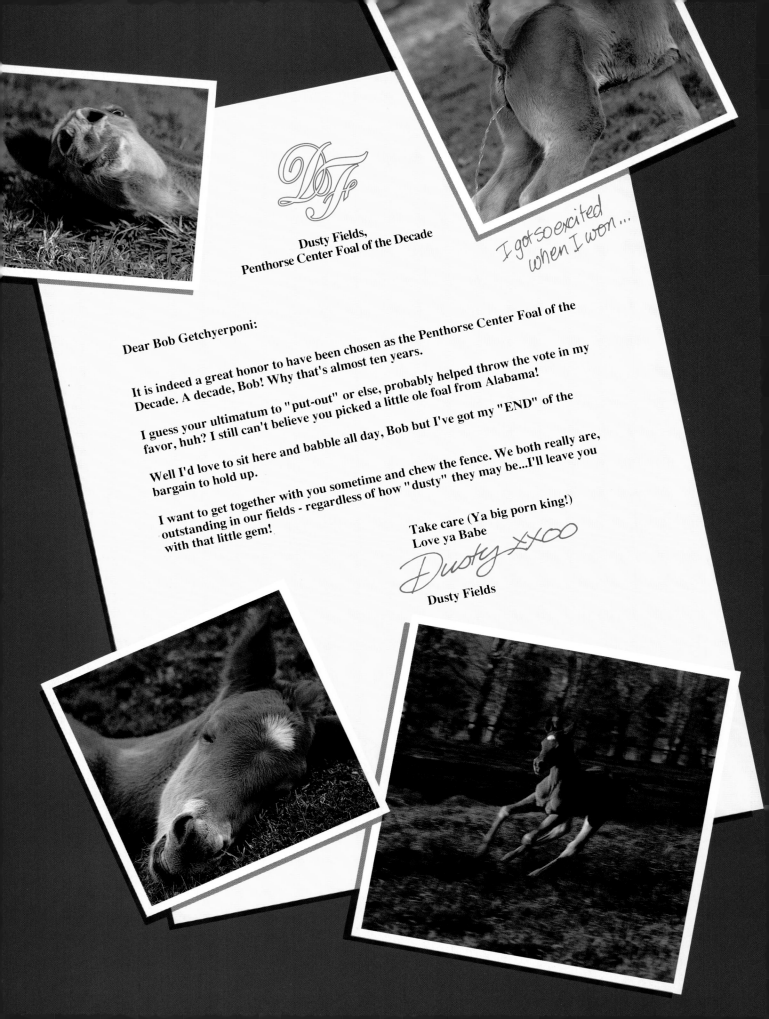

Dusty Fields,
Penthorse Center Foal of the Decade

I got so excited when I won ...

Dear Bob Getchyerponi:

It is indeed a great honor to have been chosen as the Penthorse Center Foal of the Decade. A decade, Bob! Why that's almost ten years.

I guess your ultimatum to "put-out" or else, probably helped throw the vote in my favor, huh? I still can't believe you picked a little ole foal from Alabama!

Well I'd love to sit here and babble all day, Bob but I've got my "END" of the bargain to hold up.

I want to get together with you sometime and chew the fence. We both really are, outstanding in our fields - regardless of how "dusty" they may be...I'll leave you with that little gem!

Take care (Ya big porn king!)
Love ya Babe
Dusty XXOO

Dusty Fields

FOR THE HORSE WHO'S NOT AFRAID OF HEIGHTS

MAIR JORDAN by MIKIE®

"I liked the shoes so much, I bought the company."

Mikie Jordan

NEVER LOOK A GIFT HORSE IN THE MOUTH...
and don't even think about doing a root canal.

THE HUMAN RACE

THE SPANISH INTRODUCE THE HORSE
TO THE AZTECS

HORSE THIEVES

BIRTH OF THE JUMP

CUTTING HORSE

HUNG LIKE A HORSE

A PERFECTLY LEGITIMATE EXCUSE FOR
LOSS OF AN ERECTION.

Barnyard Kipling Critiqued.

Was it Paddock? Or Haddock

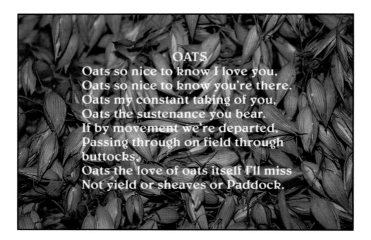

OATS
Oats so nice to know I love you,
Oats so nice to know you're there.
Oats my constant taking of you,
Oats the sustenance you bear.
If by movement we're departed,
Passing through on field through buttocks,
Oats the love of oats itself I'll miss
Not yield or sheaves or Paddock.

It's been 60 years since British writer Barnyard Kipling wrote his much applauded *Oats*. And although, for oat lovers, it still rings as true today as it did then, there has been new light shed on the work since the serendipitous discovery of the original draft. The original masterpiece (or messterpiece) was found underneath a horse blanket, in an abandoned tack box, in a deserted stable in India (where Kipling spent a great deal of time).

The original work is now the possession of Windsor Gustin, the British Ambassador to Chicago. Gustin said, from his Penthorse suite high above the windy city, "Kipling changed his mind a lot as indicated by the sloppy appearance of the original, unedited version."

Legible or illegible, the question remains: Was Kipling referring to fish (haddock) in the last word on the final line of the original draft or a small open field (paddock)? Hopefully, he was referring to

paddock because fish wouldn't have made much sense.

As the work was published posthumously (1937) and the scrawl had to be interpreted by editors, there is some speculation that the questionable word was changed so it would make better sense (some sense at all!) and, no doubt, sell better. The original version was then hidden in hope that it would not be discovered and the truth never uncovered. This was not to be.

It was either an honest, absentminded mistake or our beloved poet and author was in the process of going (or had already become) quite mad.

Evidence shows that Kipling had also written the grocery list on the top left-hand corner of the draft. At least it *was* his handwriting, but it reads as though his wife had dictated "Kippy: (My drooling little puppy) Here is the grocery list. Don't forget to pick up bananas, mango, papadums and <u>Haddock</u> (the fish!!) If you bring back another

field I'll kill you!! Don't get me wrong, I like grass, but fields don't fit in the cupboard." Had Kipling's wife forged the grocery list? Could it be possible? Was it necessary? Had Kipling himself forged it? Even less necessary!

Because there were no refrigerators in those days, shopping was done daily, usually an open-market concept where fish was widely available to anyone with ready money. So, fish could have quite conceivably been on his mind. Especially if there was some possible threat of being chastised if he forgot to purchase it.

But if OATS really meant what it meant before they made it mean what it means now, would it mean as much to us now as it meant to us before we found out what it used to mean? And if not, approximately how much *would* it mean to us? I mean comparatively? Half as much? A third as much? Twenty-one percent as much?

How is it possible that something

which demeaned so little could be *demented* so quickly by the discovery of one little *demerit*?

Maybe it was Friday. Perhaps he was just feeling fishy, and haddock found its way into his creation quite naturally and intentionally, only to be changed – intentionally – for profit.

Can't an author put F*I*S*H in the middle of a work accidentally without a reason – or perhaps on purpose – without an explanation to the masses, helping to create a little mystery in an otherwise boring world?

And, why would someone of Kipling's stature, in a relationship which in those times was normally dominated by the male, be doing the shopping?

Well, he was either pussy-whipped, in which case he would definitely be doing the shopping, or, he actually *liked* to do the grocery shopping, in which case, given the times, he definitely *was* pussywhipped. If this was the case – and let's brace ourselves for that possibility – the poem should have gone something like this:

OATS

Oats so nice to know she loves me,
Oats so nice to know she cares,
Oats so nice to do the shopping
In a market – open air!

Oats the fish I've come to fondle,
Oats a great day for a trundle,
Hope me Mrs. lets me wander
And makes my leash a little longer.
(Extra line. Use if needed.)
Oats so nice to love me Mrs. like I do
(The old Battle axe) <<<<Use only in extreme case!

We somehow doubt that Kipling would ever have allowed the above version to be published, although he did have a great sense of humor. Perhaps if the publisher caught him in an inebriated state, he might have consented on the condition that the purchaser of the work must also be smashed before reading it.

Sounds fair to me.

45

When She's Not Reigning, She's Pouring, Down At The Palace Pub!

Triple Crown is one of the Crown Jewels you can actually get hold of without encountering hunchbacks or breaking into the Tower of London. Which means that you can probably purchase it at your local store without getting bludgeoned or arrested. (Depending on the neighborhood, of course.) In this day and age, that in itself is reason enough to celebrate.

So, the next time you're thinking about slamming back a few princely libations, look for the bottle with the three-crowned monarch. It's licensed by the Royal family and endorsed by Queen Elizabeth herself.

Triple Crown

Special Old Rye Whiskey.

"Favoured around the palace...famous throughout the world!"

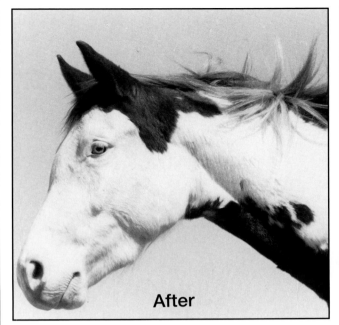

After

Before

NO SURGERY. NO DRUGS. NO WIGS. AND NO M.S.G.!

Now solve your thinning mane hair problem the natural way – without M.S.G.

The last thing you need to be worrying about when thinning hair has become a problem is Mono Sodium Glutamate.

Sure, as a food additive, it makes Chinese snappier, Italian zestier, vegetables vegetable-ier and it probably enhances a lot of other things that end in i-e-r. With the exception of words like terrier and derriere (Pronounced: Dare-E-Air) which doesn't end in i-e-r, but MSG would have little or no effect on it – at least taste-wise. Size wise? That's another story. Certainly if it did; it could revolutionize the weight loss industry and reduce the process to this: Shake it on! Peel it off! It's that simple!

With Hair Club For Horses®, there's no painful surgery, no embarrassing wigs and now, with our guarantee of No M.S.G., you can rest assured that your New Mane won't look like Chow Mein. In fact, the only sprouts you'll get are the ones that grow into a full thick mass of hair.

Our secret? We mix real horse hair in with your own. I know you're probably saying "HORSE HAIR!!! I thought that was for stuffing chairs." Well, maybe it was...but it's also great for growing hairs.

Our Fantastic Process called "Growing, Growing, Gone®" can turn a thinning head of hair into a winning head of hair – just like that.

So give
Hair Club For Horses®
a call or acquire our helpful full color brochure (so we can really throw the sales pitch screws to you in the comfort of your own stall), by filling in and returning our handy brochure request form.

Hair Club For Horses®
777 Main Street West
New York, New York

Name: _____

Address: _____

City: _____ Zip: _____

or Phone: 1-800-WOW-MANE

PORTRAIT OF A KILLER

Tex, The Cowboy-Eating Longhorn From San Antonio

"If you pick em up right the first time and get them at the proper angle they'll slide right down your throat as slick as any oyster–and a whole lot better for you too."

The Federal law enforcement agencies are convinced that he's doing it. They've never actually seen the entire procedure take place from start to finish. They have heard testimonies though, of begging and pleading, gurgling, yelling, struggling but then they were silenced.

He's even admitted to the Eatings. Murder is still a bit strong for something like this. It falls into a category under Texas Divorce law – a law that should have been updated after the sixties but wasn't. It is possibly the only thing that's keeping Tex The Longhorn out of the electric chair.

The tiny little life-saving clause reads: In the Grand Old State Of Texas . . . when one is referring to Adultery *and/or* Murder, always remember, ladies and gentlemen of the jury, that . . . Eatin' Ain't Cheatin'! (They have been lumped together like this because in Texas it has been demonstrated countless times that murder follows adultery).

Three men dead. Two of them paid in blood with their lives – the third, with the American Express Gold Card® ("Don't Be Caught Dead Without It!"). It just doesn't seem fair.

Serious crimes against humanity have been committed, yet this longhorn is still on the loose. No fence posts, no barbed wire, no cattle grids just "Land lots 'O' land 'neath the starry skies above" . . . And a legal system that can't fence him in.

Penthorse: "You're a killer?"
Longhorn: "Yes . . . Yes I am! and No! . . . No I'm not! I swallow them alive and what they do after that is their own business. My philosophy is: Never say Die! To each their own philosophy. That's what's great about living in America."
Penthorse: "But you look just like an ordinary cow to me."
Longhorn: A horse with an untrained eye. They said they were sending around an interviewer but what do I get? A horse with an untrained eye. Look it! I'm not a cow, I'm a Cattle Beast. Cows give milk. Cows low gently. Cows wander aimlessly. They come when you call them. Longhorn Cattle Beasts eat cowboys for lunch and don't you forget it. Actually I'm not even 100% Longhorn, I've got a little shot of Simmental in me too – helps bring out that hybrid vigor – but my horns are long, so I consider myself a Longhorn. Stands to reason.
Penthorse: What about the cowboy's horse, do you eat it too?

Longhorn: If they're still attached – they go too. That's why it is never wise for a horse to become too attached to his cowboy otherwise you could end up going down the tubes with him. It's not like the Navy. There is no rule specifying that "A ship must go down with its captain".

Penthorse: Yuck!!! You'd eat them both?

Longhorn: Slick as an oyster. Just four more legs to deal with and I've got all the time in the world.

Penthorse: You're a killer but you don't have a gun?

Longhorn: A gun? Ha! Ha! Ha! Ha! Ha! Ha! Ha! Ha! You *are* a very silly horse indeed. Who needs a gun when you've got teeth like these . . . (shows teeth)

Penthorse: YIIIIIIKES!!!!!

Longhorn: But I don't always choose to chew them. If you pick em up right the first time and get them at the proper angle they'll slide right down your throat as slick as any oyster – and a whole lot better for you, too.

Penthorse: But those teeth of yours are frightening!

Longhorn: Yes, and they're the last thing a cowboy remembers seeing . . . Well, that's not exactly true. They're the second last thing.

Penthorse: What's the last thing?

Longhorn: This may sound weird, but I've got this little doorman, sort of, although he's more inventory control official – I've never actually prepared a job description. I suppose I should; a job description always seems to quell quibbling. Anyhow, he makes sure that whatever I swallow gets evenly distributed to each of my four stomachs. We at Violent Cattle Beast Headquarters, give each and every cowboy kind of a last wish. They get to choose which stomach they'd like to go to. Yup! Door number one, two, three or four. It's the adult home version of "Let's Make A Veal".

Penthorse: You're all heart.

Longhorn: No, I'm not, but it's a damned big one. Certainly enough to pickle, more than enough to sink your teeth into for all you interested meat eaters out there.

Penthorse: I can't believe you'd up and eat a cowboy.

Longhorn: Oh right! I'm a scumbag because I eat a few cowboys here and there. Premeditated lunch and I'm a criminal. Look, I hate to break a good lunch engagement. I'm probably the most punctual, reliable, cowboy-swallowing Cattle Beast you'll never wanna meet.

How long have cowboys been eating Hip 'O' Beef??? Oh, excuse me . . . Bar-B-Qued Hip 'O' Beef. Does that bother anyone aside from a few radical vegetarians? They even send out invitations to their friends and neighbors. Don't talk to me about sick. The invitations are always really bovine friendly too:

"Hey, we're havin' a party! And you're invited. Just bring yourselves. We've killed a steer and it's on the spit right now. You can probably smell it from your place. But hey! Better be here by 7 PM otherwise there won't be anything left but bones! See ya when ya get here!"

Penthorse: But you're a ruminant. A regurgitator of C-C-C-Cowboys. A chewer of the cud . . .

Longhorn: Sticks and stones will break my bones . . . You can call me a ruminant or a cud-chewer or just a "Big Cud" and it won't bother me in the least . . . Just don't call me late for C-C-C-Cowboys.

Penthorse: You're sick! You're really, really sick!

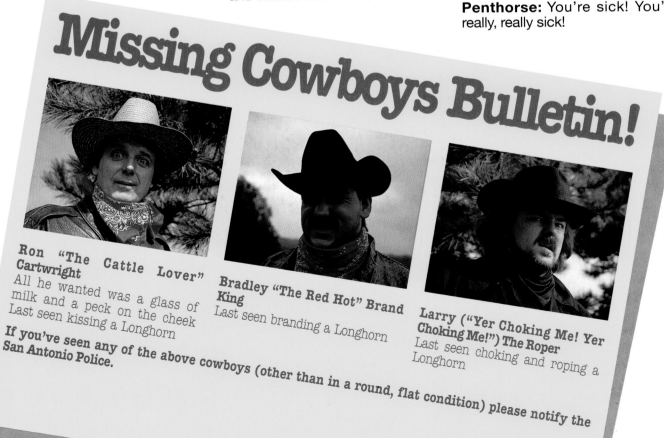

Missing Cowboys Bulletin!

Ron "The Cattle Lover" Cartwright
All he wanted was a glass of milk and a peck on the cheek
Last seen kissing a Longhorn

Bradley "The Red Hot" Brand King
Last seen branding a Longhorn

Larry ("Yer Choking Me! Yer Choking Me!") The Roper
Last seen choking and roping a Longhorn

If you've seen any of the above cowboys (other than in a round, flat condition) please notify the San Antonio Police.

At Home On The Range

The Legend Of Black Bootie

Mediocrity comes and goes - but legends never go out of style
A boot that's tough enough to wear every day is truly a boot that's
"At Home On The Range".
Don't trust your hooves to anything short of a legend.
Black Bootie...
In a class of its own!

Black Bootie ®
The Legend Lives On.

Why try to squeeze blood from a stone when you can get cash out of a fence post?

PastureCard® offers all qualifying members an endless supply of cash whenever you need it – or even when you don't. And it's convenient too. Over 9 million locations on a 100 million acres. So don't spend your retirement broke when you can spend it rolling in the clover. PastureCard. Apply for yours today! . . . We aren't sure why it works either – it just does!

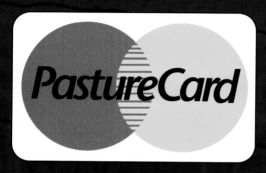

PastureCard®
. . . One of life's little mysteries.

The ASS Page

No Penthorse magazine would be complete without showing a little bit of Ass along with a brief description.
This issue is no exception.

Ass Facts:

▶ Every Ass is different. Some are as wide as others are high.

▶ Some Asses are hairier than others.

▶ How to cover your Ass: The last thing you want is a cold Ass. As the mercury drops down around the freezing point, it is recommended that you take a large blanket and throw it over your Ass to prevent a frost-bitten Ass.

▶ Crack Your Ass? At times for disciplinary reasons it is necessary to crack your Ass. This is best achieved with an open hand or hoof up-along-side-of-the-head.

▶ Pulling the lead out of your Ass: If your Ass is accidentally peppered with buckshot, it is advised you attempt basic surgery to remove it. Needlenose pliers, rubbing alcohol and cotton swabs will do the trick.

▶ Hanging your Ass out a window: In olden days, when troops would surrender they could do one of two things:
1) Wave a white flag or
2) Attach a rope to their Ass and hang it out the window.
This basically meant, "Don't shoot!...we're giving our Asses up!"

▶ A little Ass goes a long way: In 1468 a miniature Ass is reputed to have walked from Central America to the southernmost tip of South America.

▶ Sore Ass: needless to say after a long jaunt like the one above the above ass was a sore Ass – but not without a chipper outlook.

▶ *Can you tell your Ass from a hole in the ground?*

The Hunt Is On For *Elvis!*

Hunt Club Pays Graceland A Record 15 Million Dollars For Exclusive Rights To Chase Elvis.

The Hunt in Days Gone By:
Dawn Breaks

The mist has not yet lifted from the hollows. The crack of dawn is in the midst of cracking. Men, women and horses are ready. They're anxious, antsy. There is stillness. The silence is broken only by the occasional cooing of a mourning dove.

The dogs are milling about. They anticipate a chase. They sniff the ground. They sniff the air and then...they sniff...Oh No!...each other! Yuck!!

This, folks, is the main argument against allowing dogs to lick your face (even if you haven't seen them in a long while). It's just *not* right.

Friendship has nothing to do with it! And I don't think you should buy that "dogs will be dogs" excuse either.

The rule, at least in my life, is: You don't say 'HELLO' to Mr. Fudge and them come wagging over to me to play licky-face, even if it does mean, "Good morning, Master!"

I'm not making excuses for them, but perhaps this process annihilates any other odors that may be present in their nasal passages. Instead of smelling a multitude of odors they detect only one. It brings the scent process back to a beginning from which they can then go search out an "end". Would this better ready them for the hunt? Could this be what gives dogs their keen sense of smell?...I mean, after that, a blade of grass, a guinea hen, a rotting stump, a hare or "the fox" should not only be quite distinguishable from the other but they would also smell delicious!

However, if there is any truth in what you are about to read, a keen sense of smell may no longer be necessary. As long as a dog is able to identify, pursue and chase up a tree the King of Rock and Roll he will be well worth his keep.

They Ain't Nothin' But Hound Dogs – Elvis Has Hunt Club "All Shook up!" And Ready To Go

After taking much abuse and then, eventually, being outfoxed by the animal rights activists, the Hunt Clubs International have signed an historical contract which will give them the exclusive rights to chase Elvis Presley's Ghost instead of the fox.

For years they were labelled "the unspeakable after the uneatable". But if all of this Elvis stuff is accurate, they will quickly become "That groovy bunch of folks in Pinks in rapid pursuit of fun and nostalgia."

The Hunt Today

Dawn breaks in Britain, but not in the usual way. It's still last night in New York. Australians are about to live out tomorrow the only way they know how. And in Japan, they continue to make cellular phones less expensively than anybody else on earth. Looks like the losers of the Second

World War are doing very well for themselves, thank you!

But today they are already calling it "A Great Day For The British". Today the cries of the animal rights activists have been answered; they are less vocal than they were yesterday. Still very annoying, mind you, but less vocal. I always figured if we can just get them to stop singing they wouldn't be half as bad.

So where does all of this leave the Hunt Club? In a word – excited! The criticism will practically cease to exist. Their sport is now much more humane, and it will have a rhythm like its never had before…"The King is Dead!…Long Live The King!"

Some Say Hunt Club Will Monopolize Elvis

It's only been one day and already the news of the Elvis acquisition has many of the world's tabloid newspapers angry. Many wonder what they are going to tell their readers. Many are unsure of what they are going to print from here on. There are limitations to the number of 94 year-old women who can be pregnant by aliens from Mars. There are only so many per year and once they're gone, they're gone! The same goes for Yuppie babies born with Elvis tattooes.

With Elvis preoccupied (allowing dogs to rush in where wise men fear to tread) they are going to have to find real things to write about – other than Elvis.

Some concerns are:

1) Burger King sitings will no doubt decrease forcing patrons to either go to McDonald's *or* to sit there and actually eat Burger King's food.
2) There is fear that the moaning outside Graceland will stop altogether. And along with it, the already barely audible: "The Colonel *did* it and he's gonna *get* it!!!"

3) They will probably never again find a statue of Elvis on Jupiter.
4) Who is going to get pregnant with Elvis' child if Elvis isn't around to "make it shake"?

Though these complaints are legitimate, not everyone is upset.

Foxes Thrilled

"We're very pleased. We'll be able to walk around normally now, instead of as fast as our little legs will carry us. Aside from chasing the occasional rabbit, looks like it's back to straight old being "cunning as hell".

I can't say that I'm going to miss being torn to shreds although much of the blood and cruelty reported during the past two years was really overdramatized.

We had arranged a "designated victim" deal with the Hunt Club in 1989. They got to chase us all over Hell's Half Acre but when they actually cornered us, everything was halted, we would step out and the sacrificial rabbit or hedgehog was dragged in (kicking, screaming and biting) to replace us and consequently is torn to ribbons by gnashing teeth."

Ya Win Some Ya Lose Some

As with everything in life, there are always winners and losers. One certainly can't expect to please everyone all of the time. However, one thing is for certain: the hunt will never be the same. But with each and every pelvic gyration the King Of Rock N'Roll will give an old tradition an exciting new twist.

Introducing
REARING HUMAN BOOK ENDS

Humans are a funny breed. Driven by some relentless urge to succeed and to dominate, they surge forward in life; reaming, rocking, rolling, riding the waves of change *and* sticking their noses into everything…and everyone.

We at the Frankly Mint® keep our eyes and ears open for things worthy of limited reproduction. Lately our attention has come to rest on Homo Sapiens.

How else but in the company of humans could horses have been exposed to such bonuses as arrows in the neck...("Remember, we have an advantage... we have guns, they only have bows and arrows!") or a bullet in the butt...("Retreat to the safety of the hills!") or a buffalo horn in the groin...("Charge the herd - they're vulnerable!").

Yes, through the centuries humans can be credited with many an equine mishap which otherwise might not have been possible.

For this we give thanks to them and salute them enthusiastically.

Now, the Frankly Mint® has cast them - not to the wind - but in realistic, solid bronze. Why? To commemorate our lengthy friendship *and* so that you can display with pride, your favorite volumes of books, for all to see and enjoy.

This is perhaps the first time that the human race has been restricted to limited reproduction - a rather interesting form of birth control - so you better hurry; supplies are limited and dwindling fast.

Frankly®, we've never offered a better offer. Frankly®, you can't get it from anyone else, so act now!

Rearing Human Book Ends. Humans at their naked best - at last with nothing to hide. Don't miss out! Take advantage of this once in a lifetime offer!

Trust the Frankly Mint® to produce merchandise of unequalled quality not to mention a deceptively low price.

You may ask yourself "But who could afford such a product at such an inflated price?!?" If the answer is "I can! or "I can't! But, as usual, I'll buy it anyway", then fill in the easy-to-follow order form below.

Herd Times

© HERD TIMES INC.   VOL. 6, NO. 69

Fighting A Losing Battle Against The Alfalfa Lords

The cops don't have to look very far to find Alfalfa. It's pretty much under everyone's noses. And as long as horses are *chewing it* (eating it) instead of *doing it* (smoking it), strangely enough, everything seems to be okay. You can't really tell by looking. The trick to the high is in the way that it's dried.

Cut it and dry it and store it in the conventional way and everything's all right. But cure it properly, compact it into HorseHish or grind and roll it into joints; then light, puff and inhale and it's "bye-bye-car-car-with-da-da". The result, Hell On Wheels!! – Slow brain in a fast car.

The industry is both, completely innocent and extremely corrupt. It's very difficult to tell when one sees a sign reading HAY FOR SALE, who's really selling hay and who's selling dope.

Although it's commonly called hay, Alfalfa is really a legume.

We're talking very, very potent! If it's cut when it's about three feet high (approx. one meter) let dry for about six hours in a hot sun, then quickly transported to a barn and left to hang upside down for about two weeks, the

results are; not your ordinary roughage. It's *mind blast* waiting for a light.

So what are the proper authorities supposed to do? And what if the proper authorities are in on the deal, as they often are, then what? Does the government try to control rolling papers and matches? Do they introduce a tax and legalize it? They'd love the revenue but what about all the Mush Heads walking around the fields of society mumbling:

"Like *hay* man, I think I finally figured out how to, like, get outta here . . . like, man, like how to shut off the electric fence, man . . . like how to really blow this place, man . . . like *hay* man, like *hay*, like I wouldn't yank your reins on this one, man . . . Like I'm really serious this time, man . . . Like we can all be gone and this would be just, like, a big empty field, man!!!

Not exactly society at its best.

Research has shown that 42% of horses who started off on Alfalfa have gone all the way – usually ending up on molasses. Purified molasses, like heroin in the human world, is injected into a vein or artery and the results are

devastating. The governments, "Just Say Nay To Hay!" and "Say No To Moe!" campaigns have helped, but they aren't enough. If they could only cut it off at the source it could really make a difference.

South American Connection

The Amazon rain forests are being cleared for some very frightening reasons: to

grow Alfalfa and the cane which will eventually end up as molasses. The big difference: both grow ten times faster in the jungle and they're ten times more potent.

The Alfalfa Lords go about their business virtually undisturbed. Government officials who hassle them are

(Continued)

All the King's horses and all the King's men... couldn't be found for comment.

murdered.

"Welcome to the Amazon, where *membership* has its privileges and *dismemberment* has its drawbacks! Mind your own business and we'll mind ours!"

This billboard message is one of the first things you'll see when you get off the plane in Brazil. The point is clear.

The security is so tight around the Alfalfa Lords that it's almost impossible to penetrate it. The hide-outs of the Lords are so remote that they're almost impossible to uncover. If you do manage to find the location without getting picked off by snipers, there will be tanks and missile launchers to greet you at the door.

With the kingpins sitting on these kinds of arsenals the chances of taking them out – big time – are somewhere between zero and nil. Not great odds.

So the Alfalfa keeps flowing, the Lords get richer, more horses die every year, and governments around the world keep fighting a war which seems to be a lost cause.

DOES SIZE MAKE A DIFFERENCE?

The Second Annual, "Does Size Make A Difference?" Symposium finished up the final day of meetings today and organizers claim it has been a BIG *and* a LITTLE success. Using the leaky faucet analogy, they said that although some females prefer large taps because of the volume and flow, they also said once the sink was full and the tap quickly shut off, they will more often than not discover the big taps also have BIG DRIPS attached to them. They are not always the easiest things to get rid of. So it's six of one, half a foot of the other.

Once again (just like last year), the opinion of the General Assembly was that, if you're a Size Queen, indeed, size *will* make a difference, if you aren't, it probably won't.

SORRY OUR MISTAKE!

In the last issue of Penthorse, we reported that the very successful "Feed Bags R' Us®" chain was another Nags to Riches story. It should have read "Feed Bags R' Us®– Another Bags To Riches Story."

We apologize for the error and any inconvenience it may have caused.

RUDE CARROTS

Rude veggies making a comeback

Rude Carrots have been making their way from the sex pits of Bangkok into the world treat markets. These multi-appendaged veggies, vaguely resembling a reward, are orange in color, have a very sweet taste, usually followed by boisterous laughter and comments like: "Look at the stupid horse! Heez eatin' it! Sheez eatin' it! Heez eatin' it!"

Rude carrots rank high on the embarrassment scale, and decent-living horses are cautioned to carefully weigh each individual surprise to make sure it is in fact a reward and not an indecent or even pornographic prank.

ART-IFICIAL INSEMINATION: SURE IT'S PREGNANCY, BUT IS IT "ART"? . . . AND *IS* IT OFFICIAL?

Well, yes to both questions . . . sort of. Has Artificial Insemination taken the romance out of breeding? Has the art of love-making been lost? These are the types of questions sex therapists are echoing these days.

Was there any romance in pregnancy to begin with? Was there any love? Many mares will say that there certainly isn't much romance after pregnancy. There is, however, discomfort and gas and although many now believe that although gas is no substitute for romance and creativity, they are quick to add, that experiencing something – even gas – is better than nothing. This rings especially true for mares caught up in Macho Stud Syndrome relationships.

Although A.I. (Artificial Insemination) is considered to be marginally stimulating, it will not likely replace candlelight, good wine, foreplay and more-play. (Horseplay at its finest) "It is a legitimate, official form of pregnancy without all of the emotional crap" say some sex experts, but it's a long, long way from Art, love . . . and even Tipperary.

Take Superficial Encounters for instance; just because they're Superficial doesn't mean they're "Super", does it? Indeed not!

In fact, those attracted to the shallow may find their fields of love lie fallow.

THIS ISN'T NEWS BUT THIS TOO, IS REALITY.

Following the third straight newsless day in a row, we, in an effort to inject a little enthusiasm back into things, bring this special updated report on the State of Nudity in today's fragile equine world.

In addition to the above information, as well as the above paragraph, there will be a brief comment, bulletin and short diddy (note) on the frequency of redundancy in the normal daily flow of everyday conversation. This will begin with an exciting, exhilarating and gripping profile on a very wealthy, rich, billionaire.

But first the nudity question!

Aside from a few blankets here and there, the occasional parade or sudden outbreaks of pomp and pageantry, horses appear to have lived and still *do* live in a worldwide state of nudity. Horses have been able to adapt very well. Those of us who live in harsher climates have been able to react and adapt. If it gets cold we grow a winter's coat. When it gets hot, we lose it. Sound simple? It is.

Yet when Homo Sapiens evolved from the ape, as they became more ~~revolved resolved involved romantically with their neighbors spouse while he was away fishing and nibbling on grass!~~ evolved, they lost most of their coat, resulting in the necessity for clothing.

Yes, evolution and becoming civilized has been very good for the rag trade.

There are, of course, some hairy nationalities who are closer to the trees than others. One such group is the Greeks.

Horses appear to be fairly well adjusted to the nudity thing. Shame over nakedness seems to be a human phenomenon.

But as far as horses go, nothing much will change quickly. No doubt stallions will continue to present their arms (so to speak) and let 'em all hang out in fields across the country and around the world. Aside from a few snickers (and ooo's and aahhs from the female sectors) or comments of disgust by passing motorists, about the moral aspects of the practice, there isn't a heck of a lot that anyone can do about it in the silly world of human beings . . . And isn't *that* nice to know?

HAPPY "TRIALS" TO YOU, – UNTIL WE MEET IN COURT!

Ray Rogers is launching a $10,000,000 dollar envy/humiliation/trauma lawsuit against Singing Cowboy brother, Roy, and Roy's prissy wife, Dale Evans.

What A Difference An "A" Makes

Ray Rogers is a disgrace. Roy Rogers is a success and was always Momma's pride and joy.

Ray Rogers' voice sounds like domestic geese. Roy Rogers sings like a melodious bird.

Ray Rogers is a vagrant. Roy Rogers is stinking rich.

Ray Rogers eats (and sleeps) in a garbage dumpster behind a McDonald's and has been stabbed so frequently he can barely hold water (72 times – Not including 14 shots in the stomach for rabies). Roy Rogers is an American Cowboy legend and has only been stabbed twice, both times by wife Dale Evans, once over possession of the channel changer for the television, and the other time when Dale lost a coin toss to determine who was going to pay for Ray's 14 shots in the stomach. Dale was a poor sport over the incident and didn't pay for the shots for two weeks – by which time Ray was frothing at the mouth and attacking sheep, goats and cattle. So great was his trauma that even today Ray is not completely convinced he isn't a wild dog. He often lies in the driveway for days on end, chewing on bones and licking himself "there".

Ray Rogers did not stuff his horse, Trigger, after an argument. Roy Rogers apparently did.

Ray Rogers has only produced one profound quote in his life. It hasn't made him a penny of residuals. It is:

Ray's Profound Quote: "When the pitfalls of life seem to be getting the better of you, always remember . . . there's a hole at the end of the tunnel."

By contrast, Roy Rogers has written and recorded hundreds of lovely songs and has made a fortune in royalties.

Now you can see why Ray could possibly be a tad cheesed off, after a lifetime of being Roy Rogers unsuccessful brother!

Ray claims to have estimated Roy's net worth so many times over the years that he feels entitled to some of it. He wants one million for his envy suit and nine million for trauma and humiliation caused by the rabies fiasco with Dale.

AGRICULTURAL AWARENESS WEEK KEEPS POLITICIANS BUSTLING

It has been officially declared "a nice success" by bureaucrats* and banking executives responsible for making the remark. These same officials and executives also claimed responsibility for organizing the two-day, week-long event.

Next year, they are hoping it will actually last a full week instead of a disappointing two days, "Maybe chores got in the way or something?!?", said an official, Mr. Ed Gelding, who didn't want to be named.

The name given to this year's theme was: "Just Who The Heck Do You Think You Are?!? And Just Why The Hell Do You Think You Can Keep Getting Cheap Food While The Rest Of Us Are Barely Making Ends Meet?!?" The name was chosen as an attention getter.

Farmers agreed unanimously that only after food becomes unaffordable and public servants are forced to eat, Cheezie Corn Puffs, potato chips, Gumball Zingers®, beef jerky and Licorice Billy Sticks® for dinner, will they begin to grasp the importance of Agriculture. Compared to a lot of industries, it is one of life's little free-bees that ain't going to be free much longer.

Bureaucrats derived from burrocrats, meaning literally "To rule by asses".

OFF TRACK PETTING– FEELS GOOD AND EVERYBODY WINS

Chalk One Up For Decency

Well, it appears as though the moral minority has logged another definite win. It was decency, winning by two lengths over exhibitionism, in a race which left everyone speechless–and quite exhausted.

Things used to be quite different at race tracks around the world until *On Track Petting* was banned. It really is the sort of behavior that is better left at home – bring your wallet to the track but leave the moaning and groaning back at the house. Although it's really none of anyone's business what goes on in the bedrooms of this country, it *is* the racing commission's responsibility to ensure that this type of practice is confined to the proper locale.

Now that the law has been fully enforced, the atmosphere around tracks is pretty much back to normal; 97% of those horses polled feel that the intimate surroundings of the home-front is much more conducive to lovemaking than riding the rail in front of forty thousand screaming, raving, racing enthusiasts.

With racing being the largest spectator sport in the world, it made this brand of public romantic expression easily the second-largest spectator sport largely because of location. It was an annoying distraction and betters couldn't properly concentrate on the horses – some compulsive gamblers even

Continued on next page

TO SWALLOW OR NOT TO SWALLOW.
THE EQUINE JOKE THAT WENT TOO FAR

If you think those little birth control pills are just little birth control pills, *Urine* for a big surprise.

The news that pregnant mare's urine has ~~piddle~~ little or nothing to do with the formula which prevents pregnancy in humans, was leaked last night by the media. It has many women hopping and gagging mad.

It now appears as though it was slipped into the formula as a prank, obviously by some horses' ass(es). It involves the formulae of all worldwide pharmaceutical companies' products. They were horrified when the story broke. Many wondered why nobody had ever actually checked the formula more carefully. We thought that horse pee sounded a bit weird but we're in upper management . . . Who are we to argue with the so-called geniuses down in the lab?

It appears the perpetrators of the prank, all of whom are horses, came up with the idea at an annual convention on joke night. The scandal involves all chemists, on a global level!

Although the General Public* is not exactly laughing at the gag, one has to admit that it's an extraordinarily good one. A prank like this has not been seen since native Hawaiians convinced Captain Cook that eating many raw oysters (a Phlegm-like mollusk) created a condition known as priapism, (a state of perpetual erection) which would better enable them to maintain a woman in every port. Sounds to me like Cook got took.

I have capitalized the words General Public out of respect. I think it's only fair considering that a word like Nevada has enjoyed all the benefits of capitalization, yet up until now General Public has not. Let's face the facts! If it wasn't for the General Public, Nevada would still be tumbleweed and sand!

PALOMINO OR PALIMONY?
THERE IS A DIFFERENCE, BOZO!

What's In a Name?
What's your preference? Potāto? Potăto? Tomāto? Tomăto? Palomino? Palimony?

Hold it right there! Although some easy-going vegetarians may argue that it's simply a matter of whatever feels right, by mistaking Palomino for Palimony you could discover that you're a voice without a choice! A word to the wise: When it comes to these two particular words, forget the veggies and their religious followers, sound out the words and listen keenly. With Palomino, off in the distance you'll hear a horse softly whinnying. With the other, very close to your ear drum you'll hear someone screaming "You bastard! Do you call THIS a settlement!" See? Not all words are accompanied by a kiss and a promise of something nice.

If one were to choose Palomino, one could inherit a horse. A very nice horse but a horse just the same. Another mouth to feed – one more body to shelter.

If you choose Palimony, there is no prize showcase to open, there is no cash to be won, you don't even get a horse. You just pay! pay! pay!

By these examples, the importance of literacy becomes painfully apparent.

But what about the innocent? What about those who just wanted a horse? They ordered a Palomino and ended up getting served with legal papers demanding that they pay! pay! pay! Or those crazy ones who wanted Palimony and one day, much to their disappointment, a big truck pulled up out-front and unloaded a marvelous golden horse. All they wanted to do was pay! pay! pay! Where does it leave them?

Well, given that horses often come into this world looking for a nice comfortable place to die, maybe, just maybe, their wish to "pay, pay, pay," will finally come true. I mean, the vet bills alone would be enough to break them.

There was a similar situation several years ago among the middle and upper-class illiterate. It seemed that many of them could not distinguish between the words "horse" and "divorce".

Sympathizers of these groups are advised to wash their hands of the mediator role. Instead, give a donation to one or both of the following charities: The Agency For The Incredibly Dense and/or The Association For The People Who Can't Tell The Difference Between A Bloody Horse And A Tomāto. (Or is that Tomăto? . . .)

THE ODDS COUPLE
WELL EXCUUUUUSE ME!

A New Jersey bookmaker is being sued by his bride of one month as a result of a slight (major!) misunderstanding over his profession.

When they met he thought he'd be upfront with her, so he told her he was a bookmaker. The naive woman began fantasizing about being married to an author.

"I have always been attracted to that rare breed which is disciplined enough to sit down and write, to let the juices flow until – at last – it all comes to fruition," a disappointed bride told a jammed courtroom.

Without asking any additional questions, she promptly requested his hand in marriage. He accepted and off they flew on their honeymoon. The romance, if it can be called that, lasted approximately thirty minutes. There wasn't actually any body contact but there was a lot of coaxing, naked prancing, and parading about in scanty lingerie, all to no avail.

He spent every second of their honeymoon on the phone in the hotel talking to everyone from everywhere and the only thing that got laid was Bets! Bets! Bets!

After the third day, she finally screamed "Joe! What are the odds of you not coming into the bedroom and making love to me?!? I mean how does a girl like me win with a guy like you?"

Joe replied, "Well, I'll give 10 to 1 odds. So a two-dollar bet will get you twenty and I'll throw in track odds at no additional charge. If you win, and I'm sure you will, 'cause I'm still very busy on the phone here, you're looking at twenty-two bucks. Not bad for a bit of anguish and a whole buncha dancing around in the nude."

Well I'll *bet* (but not more than two bucks) that next time she looks before she leaps.

OFF TRACK PETTING–
(Continued from previous page)
stooped to wagering on the shenanigans taking place in the bleachers. Many of them were lucky enough to *win big*.

"We know that people love to come to the races and we certainly want to accommodate them, but it was getting *way* out of hand!" says Bill Smith, race track manager. "I'm not even sure how it got started but I have a sneaking suspicion it was our 'Come To The Races' promotions drive. Perhaps they thought it was the beginning of *The New Morality Era* and jumped at the chance to take the slogan literally."

"What happened to the old morality? I have no idea, but if it's anything like technology, it has to be updated from time to time to remain competitive. However, this was one update that we got backdated and so far it seems as though everyone is better off for it".

Now, folks arrive, place their bets *and* their butts in the proper places, and end up having an enjoyable time. Kissing, holding hands and schnoozling is still allowed – in moderation – but anyone who engages in radical behavior will be arrested and taken away.

THE UNDOING OF MISS A-MARE-ICA

Another "fallen angel" story? We don't think so.

Vanessa Wilkins had everything going for her. She was (and still is) a beautiful model, (you don't have to be plastic, but it helps) she had financial success, and had been chosen the most beautiful mare in all of A-mare-ica. The pride of the entire land; the envy of all the other contestants. But she wasn't satisfied with that. She wanted one more crown. She wanted to appear in Penthorse magazine, and she wasn't about to stop until she achieved her goal.

So, she sold Bob Getchyerponi (of this very publication), some incriminating negatives for a lot of money. They were kinda-nakedy-lesbianish- bit-o-this-bit-o-that-kinda-pictures. Of course, this photo session took place *long* before the Miss A-mare-ica Pageant, so in Vanessa's mind, it shouldn't have upset anybody. Well, there's nothing like turning a negative into a positive and then back into a negative.

The bottom line was, the Miss A-mare-ica folks were *not amused.* They stripped her of her crown and overnight she became a national disgrace. But she would not let this prevent her from realizing her ~~fool~~ full potential.

All she has left now from the past is a whole buncha bitter memories. However, her *future* looks extremely bright, thanks to Bob Getchyerponi and Penthorse Magazine. She has a million bucks in a suitcase and a body everyone recognizes. She's the first horse ever to host the hit television show: "America's Most Embarrassing Humans". *And*, she toys with the exciting possibility of a career in porno flicks.

How's that for turning things around in a hurry?

Penthorse Magazine can open these doors and a (w)hole lot more for you, too. For more information on how you can be a fallen angel and rise to fly again, phone: Bob's School of Flighty Characters and Advanced Eroticism, at: 1-800-MEE-2BOB.

HORSES AGAINST NutraSweet®

SWEET SURRENDER? NO THANKS!

So we run a mile and an eighth in two minutes flat – for what?! Fewer calories? I don't think so!

Because the demand for diet soft drinks has been growing in leaps and gulps with the development of the more palatable and supposedly safer artificial sweetener, NutraSweet®, the definition of the word "reward" has changed dramatically. Many die-hard sugar-loving horses feel NutraSweet® is not a substitute for the taking of lumps where lumps are due.

A spokesshorse for H.A.T.S. (Horses Against The Swirl) says the manufacturer is going to have to sweeten the deal before horses will begin taking their product seriously.

The NutraSweet® manufacturers have been "raising cane" in the marketplace with their assault on the sugar producers as well as peppering the public with their message that NutraSweet® Equals Sugar. The results: windfall profits, and outrage from their competitors.

Sugar producers have lashed back bitterly, claiming that they're misleading the public and short-changing the horses.

This negative publicity has left the producers of NutraSweet® with a bad taste in their mouths, but they claim it hasn't hurt their market share.

Ass-partame, NutraSweet's® real name was originally developed to control bad breath in Burros – hence its name. (Burro Breath! Burro Breath! Poncho's got Burro Breath!) Needless to say, the name Ass-partame was a stumbling block for the products saleability in both the horse and human markets.

BIRTH OF THE TROTS

While the Spanish were busily introducing horses to the Aztecs (February 19th, 1519) under the charge of Hernando Cortez, the Aztecs under the rule of Montezuma II (on or about February 20th, 1519) reciprocated by introducing diarrhea to the Spanish. (Hence the term Montezuma's Revenge) The Aztecs believed that if you kept your guests on the run throughout their stay, they would return time and again just to repeat the experience. They would leave behind a *lot* of tourist dollars, too. Since then, in the area of tourism, Mexico has carried on this rich and loose tradition.

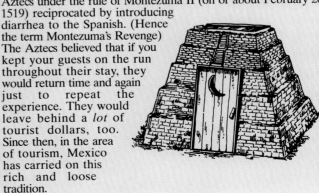

THE OAT BRAN SCANDAL

COW POOP MAKING HOLE BIGGER

Saskatoon, Saskatchewan

Several years ago, a horse could walk into any hotel, order a bucket of oats *and get it*. Well, you can kiss those Days-O-Plenty goodbye.

Suddenly, every human on earth is worried about his or her colon. Whatever happened to the topics of fresh breath, white teeth, full-bodied heads of hair and feminine protection? Suddenly all the attention gravitated to "THAT" area! The disturbing part is that everyone is soaking it up – and with great regularity.

Somebody in the world of advertising is hoodwinking the public and the public is not yet aware of it. They will buy anything and everything which has the words Oat Bran printed on the container.

Marketers have found a wonderful new sales vehicle. Take the new Playtex® push-up bra for instance. The one with the straps re-enforced with Oat Bran. Apparently, it's the Oat Bran which allows them to stretch as wide as a field of oats and still retain their elasticity, even after years of wear.

The General Motors Paint Division has developed a new stone-chip protective formula. It has a rubberized Oat Bran base which actually prevents chipping and redirects the stones back in the direction whence they came. They've patented the breakthrough and are presently licensing its use worldwide to all other auto makers. By 1993, you will not be able to buy a motor vehicle which does not contain Oat Bran. You may want to make a mental note of this if you're a corn flakes fanatic and you're in the market for a new car.

For any humans reading this, there is no doubt in my mind that we are in the middle of a full blown Oat Bran Scandal. May I suggest that you be sensible about the food you ingest, be wary of the hype and do whatever is humanly possible to leave us horses just a little bit of oats to wet our whistles now and again – so we don't forget what it tastes like . . . Thanking you in advance.

No matter how you cut the pie, the world loses.

Methane gas in cow manure has been cited as the latest cause for the widening hole in the ozone layer. Because cattle number in the hundreds of millions, it boils down to a lot of caw-caw being (literally) dumped each and every day! This has forced Environmental Officials to step up their "Eat Beef" campaign. Although red meat is not supposed to be good for your colon, *no ozone* is a lot harder on your entire system.

There was also some speculation that fresh cow poop was having some effect on global warming and perhaps it does, but only for a few minutes.

"All it takes is one itty bitty cool breeze. So if you're thinking of running out and buying a new bikini to cash in on the warmer weather – don't. I doubt that the excess temporary heat will enhance your tan to any greater degree!", said a manure expert, Mr. Dungg Heap, who asked not to be identified.

Now You Can Hop, Skip And Jump Without A Skip, Hop Or A Jump.

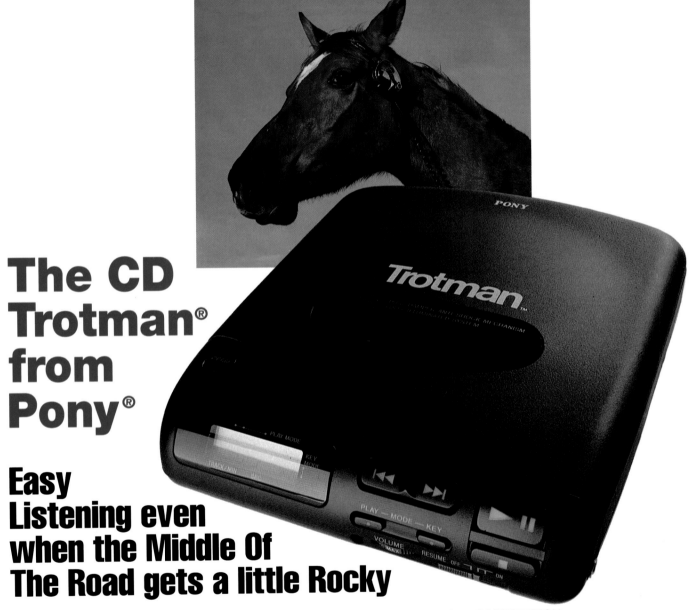

The CD Trotman® from Pony®

Easy Listening even when the Middle Of The Road gets a little Rocky

PONY® . . . We're music to your ears®
©Pony Corporation Inc.

Pass The Worms Please!

* SUGGESTED SERVING

If You Like Pasta, You'll Love Worm-A-Getti. You can trust Wiggley's, Worm-A-Getti to *get* the ones the other wormers leave behind. Whether they be stragglers or just down right plum stubborn. With Wiggley's, *once* is all it takes - and worms are done like dinner.

But there'll be no dessert for you until they're all cleaned up. So, Bon Appetite!

...It's Not Just A Wormer - It's An Entire Meal!!

Incredible Sex Discovery!

Scientist perfects amazing sex scent that makes 3 out of 4 Mares give in!

Paris - Using the discovery of two famous professors (both of whom are most likely in exile or in shallow graves [somewhere] by now), a scientist has succeeded in synthesizing the sex hormone that triggers arousal.

Then he blended it with a nice perfume and the results fall nothing short of amazing.

This amazing discovery has been the subject of critical testing and lengthy discussion in the nation's media.

It works for stallions (Sizzle #1) and mares (Sizzle #2). Works even if you've already been turned down (5 times!).

We guarantee success 3 times out of 4. Normally a stallion succeeds a paltry 1 out of 4 times.

"A Sex Scent That Turned Me Into His Slave"
(As told by Mrs. Winnie Bago, reproduced with her permission)

"Two months ago I was nibbling on some grass in a far corner of the field when a stallion came shuffling up to me. He was as ugly as a goat - certainly not my type.

He had a piece of paper hanging out of his mouth. On it he had somehow scribbled an address and, to my surprise, a short-list-of-items-of-a-grocery-nature.

Then I smelled this *incredible* odor. I was overcome by desire!

I rushed to the corner store, bought everything on the list, then went straight to the address indicated on the note. Next thing I knew, I was out of control rolling around in the hay with a total stranger. On the backs of my eyelids I could barely make out this strange flashing criptic code. Pos./neg., pos./neg., pos./neg., HIV, HIV, you dummy!, pos./neg., pos./neg. I couldn't (for the life of me) figure out what it meant. It was like my mind had gone completely haywire .... and started spewing out undecipherable messages. Anyway, maybe I had an orgasm and didn't know it!

After we were done thrashing about, he said "Thanks for coming, and oh yeah!, thanks for doing the shopping."

3 Out of 4 Scores Or It's All Free!

We have tested this formula in England, France, Australia and even Canada, of all places, where it never gets above ten below zero on a *nice* day. Then we put it to the ultimate test - The Middle East! Here, sheep and goats are *very* nervous about wandering into town on a Saturday night without their chastity belts. Now, mind you, the locals still yell catcalls and blow kisses at the sheep and goats; but they always go home with a horse.

Now, you too, can "take advantage" of this no-risk offer. Put some behind your ears, under your tail or legs and if you don't score 3 out of 4 - if they don't surrender to your sweet caresses - just write us. Tell us in your own words just what kind of unattractive, hopeless, pathetic horse you really are, and we'll send you your money back in an embarrassing, spot-at-a-glance, fluorescent yellow envelope - no questions asked!

Here's How it Works!

It's been proven that odors contain messages. For example: If you smell manure the message might be "Hey! Don't step in the shit!" The message is then received by the brain, decoded, then causes anyone to react according to the message. See? It's easy. And it's no different with sex.

Sizzle #1 and Sizzle #2 contain very potent sex molecules (Pheromones. The same stuff they put in spumoni ice cream. Why else would anyone eat something that's green *and* full of crud.) They excite the neurons that control your yes/no behaviour.

Now you can turn warm slag into a gushing volcano!

Molecular structure of the sex molecule.

The Lotsa Cash Molecule
The Mercedes Molecule
The Horny Molecule
BO   B

HOOFMEKKLER'S PEOPLE:

Hello. I'm Horst Hoofmekkler,
illustrator, writer of wrongs and drawer of pictures.
Just a friendly little threat before you turn the page. If you don't want to end
up *on* this page - don't do anything stupid. Don't get too big for your britches,
make too much money, or become too popular too fast. If you're a senator or
a judge don't take bribes, do favors or young boys.
Draw your own conclusions from this warning and act accordingly.

~HORSE D'OEUVRES~

•bit o' neck meat with
soupçon of fresh dill.

•Belgium end hide
flammande•

•clyde's-tail-'n'-
tongue wellington
with cumberland sauce•

•horseschutto
con melone•

•tournedos de nose
rossini•

•paté de bay
with green peppercorns•

•~Food for Thought~•

warning signs to listen for:
1) "well, frankly it's been vet bills, vet bills and more vet bills".
2) "as soon as I laid eyes on that horse I spotted it for a trouble maker".
3) "it just needs a nice friendly elderly couple who can really devote the time.!"
4) a bit more gamy perhaps, but I heard it tastes similar to chicken."

THE ORIGINAL CALL GIRLS®

For all of your safe sex and telephone affairs; phone The Original Call Girls®. It's *so easy* and *so* are they.

You can talk about safe sex until you're blue in the face. Why talk about it when you can be on the receiving end? You no longer need to worry about getting *The-Big-One*... Instead, in its place, you get a big phone bill. But that's easily cured - all you have to do is pay the thing, you big dummy.

So what are you waiting for? Pick up the phone and call now! The nicest horse lips in America are waiting to whisper sweet somethings into your ears.

We are the biggest and most respected* company in the business. All you have to do to *get off* is *get on* the phone and make that call.

Rest assured, our girls are always fresh. Always ready. Always on! Millions and millions serviced annually.

The Original Call Girls®...*We make your night mares come true - even in the middle of the day!*™

*But how do I know I'm actually talking to the beautiful horse in the picture and not to some nag-swayback out in east L.A.? In fact, how do I know you aren't running phony pictures and have a national network of nag-swaybacks? Horses like myself will be paying top dollar to a national disgrace and bozo recruiting center. Oh yeah! Sign me up! I wanna be first!
Okay! Calm down, we'll give you some money, just shut up and maybe we'll let you talk to the broads free. Get off our backs and we'll talk about your deal later!

CALL TINA AT
1-800-IMA-HORSE

CALL GINA AT
1-800-HORS-LIPS

CALL NINA AT
1-800-IM-YOURS

CALL SABINA AT
1-800-IM-HOTTT

NOTTIE DOTTIE

"In the moood!"

AUSTRALIAN RULES
HORSE RACING

Here come the Aussies and there go the ~~girls~~ rules

A mile-and-an-eighth is not a great distance to cover. It can be achieved in short order by a human, on foot, using the easy stroll method. On horseback, at a relaxed pace, even quicker. At an insane pace, quicker yet. If you're a horse – as many of us are – and you don't have the burden of a rider, even faster! If you own a car, it's a joke. If you steal someone else's, it's at least a brief joy ride and less than two years in prison – if convicted.

All things considered, you can see why Dustin Upsand, Australian Media Magnate and Athletic Support Giant, abandoned the tradition of merely running around in circles and created what he hoped would be hailed as; "The Ultimate Aussie Challenge", not to mention "Your money's worth and a whole lot more."

I would first like to point out that Dustin Upsand is nobody's fool. He is rich, eccentric, extravagant, imaginative and very importantly: a league bowler. This is not the first time that league bowling has crept into one of my articles; it will not be the last. It is a grossly underestimated sport demanding a wealth of stamina. It is passive, yet requires a great deal of balls, concentration, skill and aggression to play it effectively. But bowling is not the reason for this article.

There's no rules like no rules!

As usual, Australians don't like to do things the easy way if there is a harder way to be found. They love a challenge. The sport of Horse Racing is no exception.

Australian Rules Horse Racing is fashioned after Australian Rules Football. It means, in a nutshell – anything goes, mate!

It follows in the wake of the America's Cup loss. It's called revenge. Upsand's idea is simple. Create something uniquely Australian and let the world come Down Under and try to take it away from us. They must snatch the Cup on Aussie turf, playing Aussie rules, and get back home before all the blood runs to their heads!

G'day Mate! Welcome to Australia. Welcome to Ups 'N' Downs

Upsand Downs (Spelled Ups 'N' Downs) cost Dustin Upsand, nearly

$3,000,000,000 to complete. It's like a giant Disney World for racing enthusiasts and is a sizable gamble even for someone of Upsand's wealth. It is both an endurance and cultural experience that you'll either immediately love *or* hate.

One second into the race you become painfully aware that this is no ordinary event. Because the starting gates are welded shut, the first thing riders are required to do is cut their way out using cutting torches which – hopefully – they've brought along with them. Once free of the gate, it's Ups and Downs from here. It's the name of the track. It's the name of the game.

Next, there is the en route violence. Interplay between contestants includes, but is not limited to: thumbs up the nostrils. Billy-stick in the ying yang, Iron Knob in the gob, punching, kicking, biting etc.

There are many stop-off points. At each one, riders will be required to carry out a number of tasks – some of them easy, others are not so easy and some; can be *extremely* unpleasant.

Yes, it's much more than a race from point A to point B in the fastest time possible for prize money. It is an event that makes The Bong Bong Picnic seem like a . . . well . . . a picnic! The winning contestant of The Ups 'N' Downs Australia's Cup, will first be required to complete all of the following, faster and more efficiently than his competitors:

1) Cut their way out of the starting gate.

2) Sprint a hilly five furlongs to a Hospitality Suite. Here you must drink a compulsory six-pack of Frosty Foster's Lager. This is overseen by the official judge, Sir Barry McKenzie. If there is spillage, you will be penalized. Your punishment is to suck back two Darwin Stubbies (a very large beer indeed!) and two six-packs (24 oz. tinnies) of Swan Lager (the one that puts pinfeathers in your teeth).

3) Then it's another rather hilly five-furlong sprint to the Oyster Bar. Shuck a dozen of the buggers, empty 'em into your gob and it's back on your mount and try not to get a FAT* (from the oysters) or it may be difficult to ride.

Don't know what a FAT is? Ask any Aussie.

4) Then it's a twelve-furlong race in and around the fjords (brought all the way from Scandinavia at great expense). Watch out for the spear-chucking Vikings in ships. After the third and final fjord, you will come headlong into a wildlife and domestic livestock sanctuary where you will be required to (a) Lasso a Roo. (b) Maula Koala. (c) Combat a Wombat. (d) Feela Sheila. (e) Shear a sheep – (you must put the dags in a bag and mail them home to the Mrs.) (f) Jostle a Jolly Swagman and kick 'em till his billy boils (You'll come assaulting Australians with me!). It must be sung to the tune of Waltzing Matilda – a sort of unofficial Australian National Anthem.

5) You must remount and dash for another 15½ furlongs to an open billabong (a sort of oasis with eucalyptus trees). It is here where the Aussies have a distinct edge. You must sit down on the ground and attentively listen to a ten-minute recital of didgeridoo music (A very lengthy woodwind instrument played by aboriginal musicians). It is not an easy listen. The average American can only handle about five minutes before they begin rolling about on the ground begging for their Mommies. The average Brit can enjoy zero minutes before collapsing. The average Canadian, out of politeness, can hack eight minutes before breaking into a chorus of 'The Lumberjack Song' (this is to maintain sanity). On the other hand, Australians listen to it every day. It's piped into their shopping malls and office complexes. It actually has a soothing effect on them while they drive to work in the morning. I know it's not fair, but them's the rules – OR at least that's the way it is. And any Dinky Di True Blue Aussie is quick to say: "That's Bloody Hard Cheese then isn't it, mate!"

6) Then it's another dozen Frosty Foster's Lager (Big tinnies this time) and if you can still walk or if the didgeridoo hasn't permanently damaged your inner ear, you remount and sprint an easy twelve furlongs down the home stretch and across the finish line, up to another Hospitality Suite where there are another dozen shuckers, another dozen Frosty Fosters Lager, an authentic and delicious Aussie meat pie – all of which

must be consumed properly under severe supervision. Then a quick arm-wrestle with The Official Judge, Sir Barry McKenzie. Make love (Tasmanian style) to a Sheila (brought in specially from the outback). Then you must arm wrestle her, too. And if you're still standing after this, The Australia's Cup is all yours!

For those of you smarmy types who have found yourselves here by fluke or an accident perhaps, the victim of a series of screw-ups beyond your control (a travel agent, asleep at the wheel, booked you not only into the wrong hotel, but by mistake took the liberty in signing you on as a competitor in one of these races) our sincere condolences. This is reality at it's worst. International competition at it's best.

Penthorse spoke with Sir Dustin Upsand by telephone. It is difficult to reconstruct those special moments spent on the phone. Overseas connections are priceless and the printed word has its limitations.

However, for your personal enjoyment, we will endeavor to recreate,

as much of the original mood as possible. We'll try not to lose the over-the-wire banter, the hesitations, and the foreign correspondent-style, scratchy audio transmission quality.

Penthorse: Hello! Hello! Hello!

Dustin Upsand: Hello! Hello! Hello!

Penthorse: It sounds like there's an echo in here! . . .

Operator: There *is* an echo in here! Do you yodel? . . .

Penthorse: Yes I do, Operator . . . I appreciate you asking, but perhaps we'll chat about that later . . . Thank you Operator! . . . Hello, Mr. Upsand?

Dustin Upsand: Yes! Hello! Thank you! Those three words are as nice as I get!

Penthorse: What about Ups 'N Downs? It sounds intersting . . . How did you come up with the idea? . . . I'm sure our American readers will be interested to know how it all came to be . . .

Dustin Upsand: Just get your Yankee butts down here and try to take *this* cup back to America, mate!! You'll see whose gonna be wearing the gum boots after this one. Thank you, and that's really all I have to say!

Glossary of words and terms

Sheila: Aussie slang term for woman. Other international equivalents are: chicks, cougars, broads, birds, etc.

Wombat: A small, coarse-haired bear-like mammal native to Australia, which eats roots, shoots, and leaves . . . sounds like what a lot of chauvinist men do.

Koala: A small, shy, endangered bear, native to Australia, which feeds on the leaves of eucalyptus gum trees.

Roo: Short for Kangaroo.

Dags: Little clumps of sheep manure which stick to the fleece and must be removed by hand before shipping the fleece to market.

Swagman: A transient person; a hobo, native to Australia

Aussie meat pie: Australia's national food.

Didgeridoo: A very long, wooden, wind instrument played by aboriginals. You'll achieve the same sound when you blow into a large coke bottle, only the noise isn't as woody.

Tinnie: Can of beer.

Stubbie: Bottle of beer.

Gum Boots: Heavy, tall (and very convenient) rubber boots used in the area of sheep breeding.

PARTING SHOT

" All you had to say was Giddy-up but no...it was dig, dig, dig, gouge, gouge, gouge!"